# Beyond the Lesson Plan

## 33 Questions Inspired by 33 Years of Teaching

### Steve Cwodzinski

Wisdom Editions

Minneapolis

# Introduction

As I turn 61 this year, I am reflecting on all the minds and souls and hearts that have impacted me during my lifetime. The things I learned from everyone and the things I taught to everyone. I have arrived at 33 basic principles/questions that guide me, that feed me, that give meaning to my life. Why 33 you may ask? One for each of the 33 years I taught, as well as learned from, my 12,000 students.

For years I gave out my list of principles and beliefs on the last day of class. I struggled with what to call this list. For years I went with "The List" then it evolved into "Cwodisms". But I wanted it to be more forceful, more dynamic, more vigorous, yes even a little bossy. I thought about "Platitudes" or "Promulgations" or "Proclamations" or "Pronouncements". And that was just the P's! I still do not know what exactly to call, what has now evolved into 33 questions. Here they are for your consideration and contemplation, for your edification and delight. Enjoy. I hope they help you on your journey to figure it all out.

As a high school teacher, I gained valuable insights and observations about our youth and our society. I know that we as humans do best when we inspire others to become as eager and yearning as we are. It has been said that I "Taught American Government and American History for over 30 years". Most students that I had in class would say different. They would say I taught them how to lead a richer and more fulfilling life. That the curriculum was just a vehicle to take us down the highway toward our final destination: self-actualization!

That place where we have a feeling of self-worth, which comes with liberating the most powerful force on earth: the human mind.

My best lessons were never part of the lesson plan or the stated curriculum or the learning targets or the pedagogical outcomes. They were so much more! These are the stories I would tell my 12,000 students, and anyone else that would listen, over the course of those 33 years.

On the following page is my list of 33 questions for all of us to FIGURE OUT the answers to.

These questions were the lessons that were not written in my lesson plan or on any of my exams.

Never stop striving to figure out all 33.

Slowly read, ponder and reflect on each one.

Which among these 33 questions do you consider the most vital to your existence?

Which among these 33 questions do you consider the most vital to our existence?

# 33 Questions Not in My Lesson Plan

# 1. What are you doing out there?

What you do today is important because you are exchanging a day of your life for it.

I had five names by the time I was thirteen—David Keene, Steve Keene, Steve Lebo, Steve Cwodzinski, and then simply Cwod. During the 60s, I was raised in a non-traditional household by my mom and grandparents. I was twelve when mother re-married, and my new father adopted me. By the time I entered high school, I was a lackluster student searching for something I couldn't really identify. I was a totally lost and forlorn kid with no sense of purpose who was growing up in Superior, a dying port town in Wisconsin. That dying hometown was a good metaphor for me.

I began a period of experimentation that lasted through high school, distancing myself from family and becoming close to kids who were a lot more fun to be with and took more risks. My friends and I were acting like a bunch of knuckleheads and doorknobs obsessed with tomfoolery and hijinks.

I was that kid who worked at Sammie's Pizza until two o'clock in the morning on school nights, which meant I was seldom ready to learn at eight the next morning. I was losing interest in my studies. I took classes like human math (as opposed to non-human math), woodshop, power mechanics, boys' foods, and electricity—not exactly a challenging class load. My friends and I were biding our time until, well, whatever came next.

1

I was that kid whose name at the beginning of the year made teachers sigh. My reputation as the class clown, who performed at the expense of teachers and serious students, preceded me. During a term in which no English teachers would let me and my disruptive behavior in their classrooms, I took one AP class. Every day I sat outside the <u>A</u>ssistant <u>P</u>rincipal's office (AP, get it?) where my English lesson awaited me. During those moments, while alone with my thoughts, I began to ponder becoming a teacher. After all, there were so many kids like me who hated sitting in class but loved hanging out with friends afterward. I was living the creed: "Do not let school get in the way of your education!"

There were days when I thought I could be a teacher. The teachers in my school did not really speak to kids like me. They did not excite us and make us want to come back for more the next day. I started to believe that I could be the teacher we all wanted to have.

I remember walking into my counselor's office for the obligatory "What do you hope to do after high school" meeting. When I said I wanted to be a teacher, the counselor laughed and then looked down at her notes and said, "Look at your grades and the classes you take." Then she callously added, "You could never be a teacher."

She could see this statement hurt me, so she followed it with a hint of kindness. "Besides, there is no future in teaching, you're at the tail end of the baby boomers."

Eventually, I put that meeting behind me and went back to finishing my senior year with no plans, no goals and no dreams. But the idea of being a teacher remained somewhere in my brain, waiting for the right moment to re-emerge.

As a side note, I ended up visiting a different counselor who asked me why my friends said I was "spaced out." I told her it was probably because I wanted to be an astronaut. She asked me why, and I told her because my favorite time of day was "launch time." Without a smile, she proceeded to tell me that being an astronaut was a bad idea. "After all," she explained, "as soon as you're hired, you're fired." I kind of liked that counselor.

At the end of my senior year, I still had no idea what I was going to do after high school. I was visionless, purposeless, futureless.

Even worse, no one dared ask me, "What are your plans for after high school?" My life was day-to-day, lacking any depth or breadth. I was on a high-speed race to failure and catastrophe. Yet, a seed had been planted in my brain by a loving mom, her caring parents and my adopted dad. They never gave up on me or lost faith. My mom and dad tried to help me turn things around. They saw something in me that I didn't. The seed that had been planted still needed a little light, water and nourishment, but that tending didn't begin until after high school.

Memorial Day weekend of my senior year, while recklessly speeding seventy miles an hour, I hit a tree. It took the first responders a long time to get me out of the wreck. I nearly died, but those working to save my life never gave up. The ambulance took me to the closest hospital in Superior, Wisconsin, where the ER nurse looked at my condition and said, "Get that boy over to the hospital in Duluth, where he can get the medical attention he needs. He'll die here."

After a week-long coma, I finally awoke. My eye had popped out of its socket, my face was a mess, and my flattened left leg was held together by pins, pulleys and chains. Both of my knees had been shredded to the bone. I didn't know it then, but I would be on crutches for fifty-one weeks and would have to learn how to walk all over again. I also didn't know that five years later, at a wedding, I would encounter the daughter of the ER nurse who saved me, fall in love with her and eventually marry.

While confined to my back during the early weeks of recovery, I had plenty of time for some major soul searching. Because I came so close to not being able to consider anything at all, I began to consider everything. To paraphrase Kunta Kinte from the old TV mini-series *Roots*, "I was not just going to learn to walk, I was going to learn to run."

While my peers were filled with hope and busy making plans for graduation, I was filled with hopefulness and slowly making plans for rehabilitation. After my accident, which I came to believe was no accident at all, I set out to make the most of every day. I began to appreciate the little things in life. I pondered where my life had been and where I hoped I was going because where I had been heading before the accident—well, no one wants to end up there.

Why so many of us have to look death in the eye before we are willing to live life to the fullest I still have not figured out. I had been living my life, that is certain, but I had not embraced it—not enriched or enhanced it.

Years later, as I read *The Giving Tree* to my two kids, I wondered if the tree I had smashed into was my own Giving Tree that had sacrificed itself to save me from a pointless and purposeless destiny. After reading *The Giving Tree* to my grandson for the first time, I started crying good tears.

After my car accident—my awakening—I began to think about where my life had been heading. What was my purpose? What was my destiny? Why do we have to hit rock bottom before we can see the view from the mountaintop? I began to appreciate every new day and live it fully.

Why is it we must experience misfortune before we can see all the fortune? Why do those who have near-death experiences notice that the sky is a little bluer, the food a bit tastier, the smiles of their friends a little brighter?

What are you doing out there?

Do you need an awakening? A re-awakening?

Imagine if every waking moment of your life, you are living the belief that there was nothing in this world you'd rather be doing right now, or that "There is no time or place like the here and now." What if this very moment, with your next breath, your next heartbeat, you realized the importance of this moment as if it were your last?

What you do today is important because you are exchanging a day of your life for it.

I got another chance at life and decided I was not going to squander the rest of it.

Ask the mothers who have had breast cancer, or the fathers who have had strokes, or relatives who were sent into battle, or friends who have had serious car accidents—ask them about the importance of this moment.

When I was shaken to the core, a voice in my head screamed, "What are you doing out there?" I shouted back, "I Refuse to Be Bored

Ever Again!" After all, we are all mortal. We all will die someday. We do not have forever, so why is it we fail to live as if we truly understand this truth?

Refuse to be bored! This became my modus operandi, my life's mission. For you, I wish that you will never fall into that "Dreading Monday and living for Friday" routine.

This is what I learned that Memorial Day Weekend in 1976 when I awoke from a coma in a hospital bed in Duluth, Minnesota.

No one would have predicted that I would someday become a high school teacher and a state senator. Now, as I think about my high school life forty-five years later, I am somewhat ashamed, but I truly believe we are all a product of our experiences, not our purchases, and that all my good and bad experiences made me the person I am today.

For years I have told my high school students the story of my car accident. During each telling, the class is always silent. The story is not part of any curriculum, just a reminder that life is precious, so we should not take any of this adventure called life for granted. The lesson of this story, I believe, has had great impact on my students. After hearing it, students often wrote notes to me about something that had been awakened in them. They would share anecdotes from their lives or similar incidents that had happened to members of their families. I love to get comments like, "Thanks for sharing part of your life, Mr. Cwodzinski. I really needed that reminder right now."

I repeat: What you do today is important because you are exchanging a day of your life for it.

During the 1840s, two best friends—truly soulmates—lived in Concord, Massachusetts. One freely walked the streets while the other sat in a jail cell penning his masterpiece *Civil Disobedience*. One day, Emerson walked up to the jail cell window and saw Thoreau writing. The two men exchanged words, and the two simply-phrased questions produced one of the most provocative exchanges ever. That exchange would ultimately find its way into my classroom one-hundred and fifty years later.

Emerson asked Thoreau, "What are you doing in there?"

Thoreau looked up and responded to his friend, "What are you doing out there?"

Whenever I ask that question of my students, I pause and let them think about their answer. In teacher school, I was told to wait eight seconds after asking a question before moving on. I never wait more than a second, though, because I usually have way too many questions to introduce. I can't imagine sacrificing eight seconds of my class for silence.

This was always the one exception, and I repeat the question.

What are you doing out there?

# 2. What is on your undertakings list?

What is on your Undertakings List before you are on the Undertaker's List?

In 1976, from a hospital bed in Duluth, Minnesota, I asked a nurse for a piece of paper and a pen. I began making a list of one hundred things I wanted to accomplish when I got out of the hospital—all those dreams, goals and visions I had totally disregarded in high school. I was currently a seventeen-year-old wreck pondering why I'd been given a second chance, and what was I going to do with it?

What was I going to do with that chance? Perhaps make my family, friends and acquaintances proud that they knew me!

I showed the nurses my finished list comprised of challenges like hiking the Grand Canyon and diving the Pacific Ocean. I'm sure they thought, "That patient may never walk again—it's so sad seeing him compile a list of his future disappointments."

My list consisted of items categorized by how long each would take me to accomplish—five minutes, five hours, five days, five months, five years, even five lifetimes. I was not going to blow this second chance at life, so I began by setting my goals for how to get the most out of it.

Before each year's final exam, after telling students my "awakening" story, I usually ended up asking each of them to make their personal list of goals and dreams. Then I'd tell the story of a student who came in before the final exam and said, "Last night I was studying for the final exam, and I pushed aside my textbook and my lecture notes. I got out a piece of paper and started my list of one hundred things I'm hoping to accomplish in my lifetime. Before I knew it, it was way past my bedtime, and now I am going to flunk your final."

I looked that student in the eye and told him, "Ten years from today you will not remember the final exam, you may not remember this class, in fact, you probably won't even remember me. But the list you made last night may very well shape you into the person you will become."

Whenever I told my students to start making their list, someone usually would shout out, "Does it have to be typed?" That person was missing the point. But every now and then, a student would walk into class the next day with their list of one hundred things they hoped to accomplish and proudly hand me a copy.

Your personal list should not include chores and tasks like update the computer, change the oil, take out the trash or do taxes. It should be things that will change you, help you grow as an individual and make you and your life more interesting. Of course, if you have never defrosted the fridge or changed your car's oil, you'd certainly have problems. If you haven't turned in your taxes for a while, going to prison would give you a rich, new experience—but not the kind you'd want to have.

The list is a way to begin building the foundation on which the rest of your life will be supported. Never stop striving to better yourself. Liberate your body, your mind and your soul. Your life is something to be examined, explored and experienced. So, build that base!

Visit museums to the living and monuments to the dead.

Read the classics as well as the comics.

Enjoy the neon lights of Broadway and the northern lights of the Milky Way.

Go horseback riding and ride a bicycle built for two.

Spend a night in a castle as well as in a tent.

Listen to the voices of the past and hold the hands of the future.

Go to rock concerts and symphony performances.

Examine the celestial spheres above your head and the earth beneath your feet.

Climb the nearest mountain and bridge the farthest chasm.

Journey around the world and travel throughout your community.

Work on a campaign, go door knocking, write a letter to the editor, attend a town hall meeting or even run for public office!

Don't forget the joys of laughter, poetry, art and music when working on your list. Those are the things that make life worth living.

I've been fortunate to have experienced some earth-shattering, transformative days in my life—the day when I decided to hitchhike to California, when I met my wife, when I decided to become a teacher, when my children were born, when I decided to run for the state senate and when my newborn grandson grabbed my hand. The most transformative day of all, though, was during Memorial Day Weekend of my senior year when an accident resulted in my listing one hundred things I hoped to accomplish with my second chance.

I have no idea what happened to my original list, but I know where my current list is. Here are a few items on that current list that I fondly—or should I say *morbidly*—call:

## UNDERTAKINGS BEFORE YOU ARE
## BEFORE THE UNDERTAKER

Visit Normandy beach in France

Road Trip to the Florida Everglades and Key West

Juggle four balls

Learn to play one song on a ukulele

Ride a unicycle

Ride on a Segway

Parachute out of a plane

Ride in a hot air balloon

Identify twenty wild flowers

Read *Anna Karenina*

Start your list now. Make a list of one hundred things you hope to do with your life.

Fill your list with new experiences that you hope to have.

Stop reading *right now* and write down as many as you can.

See if you can come up with one hundred challenging new undertakings and experiences to strive for before you are facing the undertaker.

Consider them investments in this thing we call life.

Voltaire said, "Shun idleness. It is the rust that attaches itself to the most brilliant of metals."

Idleness is a way of *not investing in yourself.* The best investment you can make is in yourself!

You are a product of your experiences, and there is always a new experience to be had. How many new experiences have you had today?

How many items on your "Undertakings Before You are Before the Undertaker" list can you accomplish:

In the next 5 minutes?

In the next 5 hours?

In the next 5 days?

In the next 5 months?

In the next 5 years?

Every few months stop to consider these questions:

Were your adventures and investments transformative for you?

What do your adventures and investments say about your values?

Reflect upon your top adventures and investments. Then plan some more!

# 3. What will be your life's defining quest?

I turned eighteen in the middle of physical rehabilitation. Doctors rebuilt my leg and re-constructed my knees and I would eventually spend fifty-one weeks learning to walk again. Before facial reconstruction, I asked the plastic surgeon to make me look like Paul Newman, and he laughed. As a result of massive head injuries, my memory would be damaged for the rest of my life.

I found myself physically, but not intellectually, attending the University of Wisconsin-Superior. I found that my hometown was not providing its young residents with a hopeful future. As with most port towns on the Great Lakes in 1976, Superior was dying. Its mills were closing, main street was going out of business, and the middle class had collapsed. I started thinking about where my life was heading next and decided I really needed "to get out of here."

Seeking mental rehabilitation, I sold all of my possessions, said goodbye to my friends and family, and hitchhiked to Minneapolis, where I stayed at the YMCA. I may be the only person who lived at the "Y" while the Village People were singing about how much fun I was supposed to be having at the Y-M-C-A. Later in life, my two children, who were familiar with the Village People version of the song, begged me to tell stories about living at the Y. Actually, living at the YMCA in 1978 was not fun. It was, however, very cheap. Soon I moved to an old brownstone and worked at a downtown hotel. I lived in a one-room studio apartment with a friend. Our only appliances were a toaster and a small fridge. I slept on a mattress in the closet, and he slept on the couch. It was hard to save money making minimum wage, but save we did, because we preferred experiences to purchases. I was on a quest to figure out how this thing called life worked.

One afternoon, I pulled out the list I had made in my hospital bed to see how many items I had checked off. The first item on that list was *Meet my biological father.* I had never met him, heard his voice or seen a picture of him. In fact, my grandparents had forbidden the speaking of his name. They had cut him out of all the photos with my mom. But still, there was that unachieved goal listed as number one on my list— *Meet my biological father.* It remained at the top because it seemed unattainable. How was a nineteen-year-old kid going to accomplish this mighty task of hunting down his lost father?

The only two things I knew about my biological father was that he lived in San Francisco and that his name was Larry Keene. There was no Internet in those days to help with research, so I saved up some money, sold my few possessions, bought some cheap camping gear, then quit my job and started hitchhiking to California. I had four hundred dollars left to fund my quest.

My mother, Jackie, the only child of Jewish immigrants, had married right after high school. She had fallen in love with a gentile from the other side of the tracks and fled to California in 1957. I was born in 1958. Soon after, my mom left my biological father and moved back to Superior, where the two of us lived with her parents. I had not seen my father since.

Before I left to find my dad, my mother looked me in the eye and said, "If you do this, I will never speak to you ever again." I thought, *Sounds like a promise, not a threat!* (Just kidding, Mom.) My grandmother said, "If you do this, I will cut you out of my will." I thought, *Grandma, you're nearly broke.* My friends said, "If you do this, you'll miss some awesome parties." I thought, *My friends are my Gibraltar, but I've already been to a bunch of awesome parties.* Meeting my biological father had become my mission—my goal.

In early June, then, I slung a backpack over my shoulder and ventured forth on my adventure to hitchhike all the way to California. My roommate had taught me how to juggle, so I bought three balls to keep me occupied. I quickly realized that drivers were picking me up because I made them smile—who wouldn't want to pick up a juggler, a clown? I met so many wonderful people that way. Some I was only with for a few miles, and some I spent a few days with crossing an entire state. Every day was a brand-new story, filled with new experiences, adventures and the unknown. Every day seemed fresh and new, devoid of any dulling routine or predictability. Every day was time well spent. I met hundreds of people—truckers and teenagers, salesmen and stay-at-home moms, people running errands and others who were running away. A lot of characters! Some, like me, were running toward something. (Or was I really running away? What would Freud say?)

I got lonely at times, so I bought a transistor radio in South Dakota to keep me company at night. I only received AM stations, though. This was the only thing I bought during my three-month journey.

One businessman picked me up outside Lincoln, Nebraska, and wanted me to juggle for his staff. I told him, "No—I'm not that good." He offered to buy me breakfast, though, so I relented. It turns out he ran a Cessna airport and offered to fly me on the next plane to San Francisco. I declined, telling him that I had many more adventures awaiting me on the road.

And I did. After that offer, I continued learning new skills, eating new foods, making new friends and developing new insights into my species. I backpacked in Yellowstone with Germans, rafted the Colorado River with Norwegians, surfed in the Gulf of Mexico with fellow hitchhikers and camped on a beach near the Pacific with a family from Italy. I marched alongside Bonnie Raitt and Jackson Browne (or was it Jesse Colin Young) at an anti-Nukes rally in the Black Hills. I got stuck in a foot of new snow in Colorado and was saved by a nurse—a perfect stranger—who opened up her home to me. I relied on the kindness of strangers for an entire summer. I romped in places I had never heard of and roamed through places I had only dreamed of.

Forty years later, I still think about some of those kind and caring strangers, some of which I only spent a few moments with.

Many people who picked me up told me, "I wish I had done something like that when I was your age." Whenever I'd hear this, I'd wonder, *Well, why didn't you?* But I never asked. I could usually speculate on how they would have answered by the look on their faces and the longing in their voices. Many of these people regretted having not seized the chance for adventure, and now, while sitting next to me in their car, they perhaps knew it was now too late.

What have you been wishing for and wondering about?

Which of your personal mysteries would you like to see solved?

Do you have any major regrets you could now make right?

Is there something you have been putting off, or dreaming about, that you could do right now?

Finally, after two months on the road, I made it to San Francisco. Having checked into the local YMCA, I headed for a phone booth, opened the phone book and looked up Larry Keene, my biological father. I quickly found his name. He was living in Oakland. I deposited a dime to call him but immediately hung up. After nineteen years leading up to this very moment, I had never decided what I would say when my father answered the phone. Would I just say, "Hey, Dad, want to play catch?" Or maybe, "Can I have the car keys?" Or maybe anger would overtake me and I would say, "Where the hell have you been?"

I grabbed my dime, stepped out of the phone booth and went sightseeing—which I proceeded to do for five days as I worked up the nerve to make that call. On day five, I was running out of money and had just enough to get home. This was going to be the big day.

I went to a phone booth and dialed my father's number, which I had memorized.

A man answered.

I asked, "Is Larry Keene there?"

"Speaking."

"This is Steve," I said.

After a pause, my father said, "I've been expecting you."

He gave me directions to his home, and I headed to Oakland. I spent a week with him, which helped me fill in many of the missing pieces of my life.

At one point, I asked him, "What did you mean when you said, 'I have been expecting you?'"

He replied, "I've been expecting you for about a year now. I knew that as soon as you became an adult, you'd show up someday."

After a week-long visit, I headed home. Over the years, my students have asked me some very insightful and caring questions— especially about this milestone in my life. They've asked:

What were you expecting of your father?

What do you wish your mother had told you?

Did your dad give you any pearls of wisdom?

Have you kept in touch with him?

If he had always been a part of your life, how would things have turned out?

An unexamined life is not worth living, indeed. I have told this story to my students for years. After one of my tellings, the captain of the football team came to me after class and said, "That was a really cool story, but you could never do that today."

"You may be right," I said. But I was thinking, *This kid is going to spend the rest of his life rationalizing why he should not try something new, take risks, or do something that makes no sense.*

I told my wife that a football hero, known for his courage and physical exploits on the field, had told me it would not be safe to hitchhike today. She looked at me, shook her finger and exclaimed, "If you'd had that outlook and that attitude when you were his age, you would not be who you are today!" Then she added, "It may be even more dangerous to spend your life just wishing and waiting and wondering."

That experience—finding my dad—like all my experiences, shaped me into the person I have become. I learned that you regret the things you didn't do much more than the things you did.

After sharing this story with my students, I often ended with these questions:

What will be your life's defining quest?
What will be YOUR GREATEST STORY?
Will it be among the GREATEST STORIES EVER TOLD?

I now wonder what my greatest story is. Maybe it has not happened yet. I don't think I'm too old for another adventure.

# 4. What will be your dying words?

The opening icebreaker at teacher workshops and seminars is often to pose the question, "Why did you become a teacher?" At many such events, I remember listening to my fellow teachers discuss another teacher who had made a difference in their lives—a grade school teacher who made them feel like a standout, a middle school teacher who never gave up on them, a high school teacher who ignited an intellectual spark, or a teacher who inspired them to become a teacher. Unfortunately, I never knew how to answer. I'd think hard—yes, I had some wonderful teachers, but few who truly made a difference to me. One day, when pressed to give an answer to this question, I told the following story.

I was twenty-three years old, well into my sixth year at the University of Minnesota. I was floundering, having amassed dozens of credits from classes in which I learned nothing, mainly because I was not intellectually or emotionally ready for what the professor was professing. When consulting my advisor, she threw my transcripts onto the table and began to pour over them.

"What's my quickest route out of here with a degree?" I asked.

"You already have more credits than you need to graduate," she explained. "But there is no rhyme or reason to the courses you've taken." Then she added with a slight smirk, "Is this accurate, that you have had seven declared majors?"

I said nothing.

She stared at the mess for quite a while and eventually declared, "You could earn a degree in education in a year."

"Sign me up," I enthusiastically replied. Walking out the door, I recalled that brief appointment I'd had with my counselor in high school. It may have been the most important moment in my life, though at the time I hardly took notice. Sometimes, the most momentous and significant moments in our lives slip by, but we are too busy to notice.

I became a social studies teacher. Confucius said, "Choose a job you love, and you will never work a day in your life." In my case, I guess the job chose me, and I have never worked since.

How many of us are living that adage by Confucius?

My high school counselor did not see in me what was lurking somewhere in my personality. My college advisor just stumbled upon my quickest way to a diploma. I had known all along that I wanted to be a teacher, but there were far too many imagined obstacles. Although I cannot explain it, I believe teaching was my calling—a natural fit. I would be able to challenge the young scholars who were heading off to Harvard as well as the knuckleheads (like me) who were heading off to who knows where. I loved teaching.

Sometimes, the most significant moments in our lives slip past. We tell ourselves there will be other days, yet today may be the only day to make something happen. Many of us wish our lives away, dreading Mondays, counting the days until Friday, and planning our vacations and our retirement in between. If you must say "TGIF," say "TGIM" or "TGIW" as well.

I recall one occasion on which I delivered a commencement address at the high school. When I was done, the students gave me a standing ovation. The school board, sitting behind me, were joyfully murmuring how they had never seen the students give a standing ovation to a commencement speaker before. A member of the school board whispered to me, "Never forget this moment."

Why do we have to be reminded to take notice of moments like that?

What is an example of a time when you stood back and took notice of an important moment that you may otherwise have missed?

What has been your most significant un-noticed moment?

I never regretted a Monday or looked forward to a Friday in my thirty-plus years of teaching. I had decided that I was not going to squander my existence wishing my days away, dreading Mondays and living for Fridays. TGIF has never ever been uttered by my lips.

Why do some of us squander our existence?

Sometimes, I have found myself saying, "I was at work today." But when I notice myself saying things like that, I pause now—it just doesn't sound right. It sounds strange, awkward. Teaching at a high school has never seemed like work to me. I never "went to work" in over thirty years. "I have never worked!" is closer to the truth. When I think of it, I have enjoyed every job I ever had. Pizza maker, hotel gopher, building maintenance worker, grounds crew, dog truck, garbage hauler and finally, teacher. As I begin my next career as a state senator, I have yet to say, "I was driving into work today."

I loved all my jobs.

I took three sick days in thirty-three years because, I believe, I loved my job so much, my endorphins and antibodies kept me healthy—but that's for medical professionals to figure out. (I must admit, though, that I did miss a month due to some major back surgery.)

Do you know why anteaters never get sick? Because they are filled with ant-i-bodies! But I digress.

I once worked the dog truck at the University of Minnesota. No one could believe I loved my job. My colleague and I would drive around a flatbed truck visiting all the research centers and medical experiment facilities and pick up dead animals. The local pounds and humane societies would send the university their live animals, and we would pick up the dead ones when the researchers were done with them. We picked up bags and bags of dead mice and rats. We picked up bags and bags of cats and dogs. Occasionally, we even picked up a monkey. It should have been the most depressing job ever, yet I loved every minute of it. It was, perhaps, the most interesting job I ever had.

After my shift was over, my clothes would be covered in splotches of dried blood, but still, I would grab a turkey leg and stand outside Folwell Hall hoping that my new girlfriend would come out the front door of the building and see me just "happening to walk by." I was sure she would be glad to see me. Often, though, she didn't show up. I found out later that when she saw me there in clothes covered in blood and animal remains, she'd go out a side door.

I once drove the "puke mobile" to school for a few months. Here is how that car got its name. One day as I was walking with the vice principal after a faculty meeting, he said to me, "You are as white as a ghost."

I was. And I felt terrible, so I jumped in my car and headed home. You know how you get a warning that you're about to puke? Your stomach starts rumbling or your guts begin convulsing. This time, going sixty miles an hour, I vomited with no warning at projectile speed! The puke covered the windshield in front of me. I took my foot off the gas and used my hand to clear the window as I slowed down. I glanced at the driver alongside me in the left lane, who was looking back at me in wonderment. I'm sure he told everybody he knew what he had just seen. When I finally pulled over, I was covered with vomit. I'm getting sick just writing about it now. I cleaned the inside of the windshield well enough to see and drove the rest of the way home.

My wife was home, so I rang the doorbell. She opened the door, took one look at me, made me take my clothes off on the porch, and then I jumped into the bath. Then she went out to the car with a bucket and cleaned it. Now that was TRUE LOVE! She did a great job cleaning up what would later be given the monicker "Puke Mobile."

This happened during winter. A month later, the spring arrived with a sunny, hot and humid day. After school, I was about twenty-five feet away from my parked car when I first smelled that unmistakable odor. All the vomit that had leaked into the vents and crevices had been reborn in the heat of the day. I opened the door and OMG! As other staff left the building, they all got to relive my infamous "PUKE MOBILE" story.

My students always loved that story. I'm not sure why. I think they liked me saying puke chunks and puke mobile. Or maybe, it was because they knew it would not be on the test.

That my wife, Patti, would date a boy who worked the dog truck and a few years later clean out a car filled with puke chunks is a remarkable testimonial to love. I am grateful that I noticed her—or that she overlooked my bloody pants.

Queen Elizabeth, who conquered worlds and amassed fortunes for herself and her country, said this as she was dying: "All of my wealth for a moment of time." What do you think she would have done with that extra moment? Sometimes we realize too late that once a moment is gone, you can never get it back.

Would it not be wonderful if all our dying words were: "I was there. I did it all. I lived!"

That would be possible, plausible, and probable if you simply followed the three "Ls"—Love the Life you are Living!

I was always able to fit into my curriculum a favorite story about Thoreau and Walden. The two men fled the comforts of town and escaped to Walden to flee the "masses living quiet lives of desperation, struggling to get rich and buy things." I used to recite this quotation three or four times in class until heads began to nod in agreement. Then, smiling, I would ask: "Where were the masses, and what was there to buy in Concord, Massachusetts, in 1845?"

I recently visited Walden Pond where Thoreau went to get away from everything and reflect on his purpose for this planet. A cabin rests on this site today, and a large sign that reads: "I went to the woods because I wished to live deliberately, to front only the essential facts of life, and see if I could not learn what it had to teach, and not, when I came to die, discover that I had not lived. I wanted to live deep and suck out all the marrow of life…"

What will be your dying words? What do you wish them to be? When Emerson asked Thoreau, "What do you do out there all day at Walden Pond?" He replied, "So that when I come to die I discover I had not lived." When I taught this to my students, I say these thirteen words three times slowly and quietly. So, they sink into my student's souls. Then I ask, "Will any of us here today have our dying words be "I LIVED!"?

Where is your Walden?

No one, I believe, wishes their dying words will be, "I wish I had watched more TV, spent more time at my computer or mobile device." I think you would want your final wishes to be things like having spent more time with friends, read more books, taken more walks, traveled to more destinations. If your dying words are going to be filled with "should haves" you are undoubtedly having a pretty "should-y" life.

Speaking of dying words—last summer my aunt was in hospice hooked up to a machine that was keeping her alive for another few days or weeks. As she rested peacefully, I walked up to her bed and her eyes opened so I could show her a picture of my six-month-old grandson. Smiling, she said in a barely audible tone, "Isn't life wonderful?"

Fighting back the tears, I thought, *Yes, indeed it is.* She died the next day.

What dying words do you hope to avoid?

What do you hope will be your dying words?

# 5. How many days do you have left?

**M**emento Mori!

    During the Middle Ages, monks used to greet each other in the monasteries with the salutation, "Memento Mori!" Translated, this meant, *Remember that you must die*! These days, if I said to a student, "Remember that you must die!" there would be a lockdown at the school. My, how times have changed. However, what a nice daily reminder that salutation is—a challenge to make the most of every day and a reminder that we do not have forever. This is what I came to realize after I almost died in my car accident.

    One of the most unusual props I used in my classroom was a tombstone with "Everybody will die, yet not everyone will live" inscribed upon it along with the date, "1958–?" I was born in 1958, a morbid reminder for me and possibly something more than a prop for my students. I used that prop from time to time to remind myself, and my students, of the importance of that dash between our birth and our death.

    I often asked my students what the dash between their births and deaths would be comprised of? For me, instead of the inscription "1958–2038," what if was changed to "1958–I Lived–2038?" Would you live your life differently if you knew how much time you had left?

    Next to the tombstone in my classroom hung a 6.5 x 2-foot-long horizontal banner. I called it a LIFE LINE! I'd hold up a piece of paper and declare it to represent one day of a student's life, and then hold up seven pieces of paper representing one week of a life. Finally, I'd hold up 365 slips of paper announcing that these represented one year of a student's life.

Pointing to the banner hanging from the ceiling, I would add, "If I had eighty piles of 365 pieces of paper, it would visually illustrate the number of years you may live. And if I put all eighty piles on top of each other, you'd get a pile over six feet high." This was the length of my banner, assuming we will make it to the age of eighty. If any student would make it to eighty, he or she could greet the people who showed up at their party like a pirate once did to his guests, saying, "Aye, Matey! I'm Eighty!" But I digress.

There were vertical lines drawn on the banner depicting the major turning points in my student's lives. If you take 365 pieces of paper, it will pile up to about two inches, and so there was a line drawn on the banner at two inches. Another line appeared at about thirty-six inches, about the time a student entered high school. At forty-four inches, a line was drawn where a student would graduate from high school. I would usually point out on the banner where I was on that particular day—obviously much closer to the end then my students.

Then again, I would hold up a single piece of paper and reemphasize that it represented one day. I would tell the class that once this day was gone, they could never get it back. They might say, "There will be other days," but then I'd point back to the single slip of paper in my hand and say, "This may be your only day! What will you do with it?" Sometimes I would add, "Will this be a great day ending up in your trophy case, or in your scrapbook, or on your mantle—or will it be a day ready for the trash?" And with that remark, I'd crumpled the paper and threw it on the floor.

Would this day be a Thesis Statement Day?

Or would this day be a Feces Statement Day?

If I could have, I would have held up 28,470 sheets of paper—but instead, I used the banner. Some knucklehead would usually ask if the banner included leap year days.

I'd point at these lines/benchmarks on the banner and ask, "How are you doing so far?" Then, pointing to the last line, I'd say, "This is coming up quickly—it's the moment you graduate, and 20 percent of your life will already be gone."

That statement really resonated with my students. They were surprised by that simple fact. Most had never thought about it. I would follow up with: "What will you have to show for all this time that is already gone?" This was when I'd often point out again where I was on the banner and do a little self-reflection in front of the class. What did I have to show for all those days and weeks and years that I had lived? And what did I intend to do with the shrinking number of days I had left?

"You see," I'd say, gesturing at the hanging banner, "this is your life!"

Sixty years from today, seniors will be winding down their life and wondering where all the time went. What if on the day you were born, your parents gave you a day-by-day calendar like the ones where you rip off each day to reveal the next one. But this calendar would be over 28,000 pages long. Every day of your life, you would rip off another day and stack it alongside the calendar. As the pages of that calendar diminished and the discarded ones piled up, would those remaining pages start to seem a bit more precious?

I wonder.

Get a sheet of paper.
This is your day, what will you do with it?
This *was* your day, what did you do with it?
Get seven sheets of paper.
This is your week, what will you do with it?
This *was* your week, what did you do with it?
Get 365 sheets of paper. Ok, maybe just imagine that many.
This is your year, what will you do with it?
This *was* your year, what did you do with it?

Having just turned sixty-one, I am getting closer and closer to the end of that hanging banner.

One year, our school bulletin started announcing how many days were left in the school year. While reading the morning announcements, I would read the number of "Days Left" as the school counted down from 21 to 20 to 19 to 18. When the day arrived that the bulletin stated "17 days left", I entered my classroom outraged. I began class by simply lecturing, which led to some yelling, and finally, some screaming about the obvious message this countdown sends our students.

The clear message was that there were only 17 days of hell and teachers and books and bells and homework until, in each student's mind, "I can do whatever I want, whenever I want, wherever I want and however I want."

The veins were bulging on my neck, and I was spitting everywhere as I shouted out the message: "I am not enjoying the present, and I cannot wait for the future." I was on a five-minute rant.

One senior, 17 days from graduating, was sitting in the back of the room. Slowly she raised her hand as if I would rip her arm out of its socket if she raised it too quickly.

I yelled, "What is it?" upset that she would dare interrupt my diatribe.

She said, "Maybe the administration was telling us how many days were left so that we would make the most of every day—like say hi to our best friend from middle school that we have lost touch with, or to say hello to that person we never really acknowledged, or maybe thank a teacher for reaching out to us, or possibly get that B+ in math up to an A. Maybe that's why they are reminding us there are only 17 days left."

I was amazed by her refreshing attitude. In fact, I was speechless. I was stuck inside the box, seeing things through my foggy, cynical, pessimistic eyes. I had lost focus! Put on those rose-colored lenses, she seemed to be saying. Do not rush time—it is the most precious thing we possess.

This was the day the spit free zone was created. By the end of my rant, pre-spit free zone, students were holding up their books, binders or anything they could grab to avoid getting sprayed with the spit from my yelling and shouting. The next day I had my desks arranged so that there was a large empty space as students entered my room, which now had grey duct tape marking the floor. The tape was intended to keep the students a safe distance from my tirade's spittle. I had created what became the "spit free zone."

I once had a senior on the last day of school tell me, "All year, I could not wait for this day to come. And now today, on my last day, I find myself wishing it would never end."

The greatest thing I can do for my students, colleagues, family, friends, neighbors, fellow state representatives and senators—in fact, everyone I come into contact with—is to not fall into that "countdown" routine—whether it's counting the days until vacation, graduation, retirement, the end of a session, or simply this Friday. When we count the days, we lose the meaning of the moment.

This moment, right here and right now, matters. In fact, it may very well be a defining moment in your life—perhaps *the* defining moment of your life.

Enjoy and savor this moment. Make this the best moment ever. Memento Mori!

Once a moment is gone, you can never get it back.

I once overheard a student in the hallway say this: "I have an hour to kill." That expression is like fingernails on a chalkboard—or for younger people, "Permanent marker on a Smart Board." I thought about what the student had said for quite a while.

Finally, in class, I went on another rant. "An hour to kill!" What was he thinking. He should have said, "I have an hour to *fill*." If he just wants to kill time, the most precious thing we all possess, does he understand I've had a few students die? I wonder what they would do with that extra hour that he wanted to kill. I bet with sixty minutes you could change someone's life, have an epiphany, write a letter, or read a short story. Imagine what you could do with just one hour?

I've had far too many students who have died over the years from diseases, accidents and mental illness. One student went home around noon with a headache. At three, his mom took him to the hospital, and at six, he was dead.

I wonder what my students who have died would do if they could come back for just one hour.

What would they tell us, what would they want to do, who would they want to be with?

I wonder what they would say about road rage and revenge.

I wonder what they would say about video violence and mindless massacres.

I wonder what they would say about grudges and grievances.

One day, as I was walking into school after a long break, a teacher said to me, "I hope the kids are all rested." I nodded and continued walking to class. When the bell rang, I told my class what the teacher had said to me, and then my tirade began.

I told my students, "I hope you are not rested. I hope you are exhausted. I hope you are dog tired. I hope you are wiped out. I hope you spent your break constantly going, constantly moving, constantly growing. Rested? You can rest when you die—that's when you get to proclaim, 'Rest In Peace.' Until then, *live*! You are not amoebas, or protozoans, or single-cell plants—you are homo sapiens, creations of the highest intelligence. Your ancestors did not crawl out of the primordial swamp for you to chill. And we are the ancestors of generations not yet born. I will say it again—we are the ancestors of generations not yet born! What do you hope to leave for them?"

When my kids were little, they once made the mistake of telling me, "I'm so bored." I took them into the office where we had hung a wall map of the world. I told them that being bored is unacceptable. I asked them, "What's wrong, is there nothing to do on planet earth today?" I exclaimed, "Boredom should never be an option!"

They never said, "I'm so bored" again, at least not to me.

One of my favorite poems to teach was by Edna St. Vincent Millay:

My candle burns at both ends;
It will not last the night;
But ah, my foes, and oh, my friends–
It gives a lovely light.

Our jobs as teachers, parents, neighbors, friends, peers and perfect strangers is to build an enthusiasm and exuberance for every waking moment.

Time is so precious. What is wrong with us? Why do we not understand that the expression "I have an hour to kill" is a slap in the face of all those who have preceded us—and to all that will succeed us?

What would your perfect hour look like?
What would you do if you knew it was your last hour?
How many days do you have left?
How many hours?

Memento Mori, truly!

# 6. How interested (and how interesting) are you?

**A**re you interested?
    Are you interesting?

I have been asked over the years, "What was the first thing you crossed off your list?" I have no memory of that, but I do remember the last item I crossed out.

In class one day, I was telling my students about the list I had made in that hospital bed. A student asked me if there was anything on my list I had not yet accomplished. I thought for a minute, then told the class that I still had not ridden a horse. That was the only item left from my original list. (I did not think the pony ride carousel at the county fair counted.)

Toward the end of the school year, the student who had asked that question came to me after class. "What are you doing this Saturday?" he asked.

I told him I was busy.

The next week he asked me again, "What are you doing this Saturday?"

Once more, I told him I was busy.

The third week he stopped by again and asked me what I was doing that weekend. Again, I told him I was busy, but this time he persisted, saying, "Are you just saying you're busy, so you don't have to find out why I'm asking?"

I looked at my student with an "I am so busted" expression and finally came clean. "Yes," I admitted.

He said, "I have a horse ride set up for the two of us this Saturday morning at ten, and here are the directions. I'll see you there—my treat."

To this day, that is the only time I've ever been on a horse—and I loved every minute of it.

The more you explore, the more you will find things that need exploring.

The more you examine, the more you find what needs to be examined.

The more education you get, the more education you will discover you need.

The more exploring, examining and educating of yourself you do, the richer and wealthier you will become.

I used to tell my students to not let school—the cells and bells and bricks and mortar—get in the way of their education and enlightenment. Young people need to get out of their seats and into the streets. Our youth need self-exploration time—not in front of a screen, but in front of and before the world. In recent years, play zones have shrunk. When I was young, we would leave after breakfast, a bag lunch strapped to our bikes, and then be home for dinner. Today, if our children do not check in with us every fifteen minutes, we adults freak out. We need to get out of our comfort zones to realize all the possibilities that the world presents to us. We need to expand our walls and answer the calls we are receiving—especially the call of the wild.

So, what are you waiting for?

When did you last feel a sense of wanderlust?

After I returned from my hitchhiking adventure, my friends had a party for me, my mother decided to talk to me again, and two years later my grandmother passed away and left me four thousand dollars. I had thought she was broke. My friends said: "Look, now you can buy a car and get your driver's license." I had not driven a car in over four years, not since my accident. I thought, *Is this what I want to do with my money, buy a car?* I flashed forward fifty years to when I had grandchildren. "Come sit on Grandpa's lap, kids, and hear the story about the time I bought a car."

I thought not.

I grabbed my camping stuff, went to the airport and bought a round trip ticket to London with a return ninety days later. At the age of twenty-one, I went vagabonding through thirteen countries for an entire summer without knowing a single soul. While my friends said I would miss some awesome parties, which I am sure I did, I was able to touch the Berlin Wall, gaze up at the Sistine Chapel, taste authentic Greek food, hear the sounds of the London Philharmonic at the foot of the Acropolis, solemnly gaze upon the ovens in a concentration camp, smell an ocean breeze in Portugal, and hike in the Swiss Alps.

It was quite an adventure. In fact, it changed my life. I met other young people who were searching for meaning, for fun, for adventure or for their historical roots. We were all searching! I made so many wonderful new friends.

Shortly after my return, I met the girl that would become my wife. A few years later, we got married, and she quit her job. She wanted to go on an adventure like I had, she said. She had been to the Soviet Union, Germany, Italy and Scandinavia for shorter trips, but she wanted a true adventure, one lasting months.

I was already teaching, so I had summers free, and she was ready for a major adventure. Our friends thought she was nuts—after all, she was making more money than me, and we definitely needed a deck on our house. I told her that I had spent two summers living out of a backpack, so this time I'd rather spend a summer living out of a car.

On the last day of school, we packed up and set out for Alaska. It was an amazing three months! We touched glaciers, heard whales breach, saw the sun *not* set during the summer solstice, smelled wildflowers and were chased by grizzly bears. Ok, I am kidding about the grizzly bears. We lived in a tent for ninety days—all right, we did get a room on four occasions because we had discovered old, unique, significant, historical, and authentic Alaskan hotels that we just had to try out. To be gone for three months involves plenty of fun and frivolity, but sometimes it was a hassle and an inconvenience. The word "travel" comes from the French word "travail," meaning strenuous mental or physical exertion—like exploring Alaska for three months.

Among the highlights of the trip was backpacking the forty-mile Chilkoot Trail that gold miners established in 1898. It is considered the "longest museum in the world." A hundred years later, it is still strewn with remains from the miners. It was in these gold fields of Canada where the miners—after weeks of strenuous work, and stuck in cramped living conditions with no baths—they would finally exclaim, "EUREKA!" This must have been where that famous phrase was coined, when someone first shouted, "You-reek-a!" But again, I digress.

We drove the Corolla sixty miles down a precarious, one-way road to a raging river. We had to pull ourselves across on a tram, then hike, then finally pull ourselves on another tram across another raging river. After yet another hike, we arrived at the ruins of the Kennecott Copper Mine.

Clearly, this destination was not the point of our journey. We wandered there because we wondered.

Another highlight was camping at Wonder Lake in Denali National Park. When we arrived, fellow backpackers told us they had been there a week and had never seen the majesty that is Mt. McKinley because it had been shrouded in clouds. We pitched our tent just in time because the mosquitoes came out. Worst mosquitoes ever! We could not even eat. If we opened our mouths, a swarm of mosquitoes would fly in. So, we climbed into our tent, wondering if we would see the mountain in the morning.

I got up in the middle of the night. The clouds had parted, and the alpenglow was dimly lighting the mountain. It was one of the most beautiful sights I have ever beheld. A transformative moment!

So, cultivate a sense of wanderlust—you will have plenty of time to chill when you die.

Get off your duffs, grab a duffel bag and go exploring.

I've often told my vagabonding stories to my students, hoping one or two may get that wanderlust bug. It was not part of any curriculum or any lesson plan. However, I believe with all my heart that it is necessary for us to seek out what is beyond our knowledge and experience—to find out what is beyond the bend.

When our children were little, we traveled every summer in a VW camper bus around Canada and the United States. One time, we were on a one-way, one-lane, unpaved wilderness road going through Redwood National Park when we got a flat tire. I got out of the van and screamed with joy and rapture. Our kids asked their mom why Dad was so happy to have a flat tire in the middle of nowhere. In a worried voice, she honestly replied, "I'm not sure."

I explained to the children, "Because I get to change a flat tire under trees that are over a thousand years old. I must be the luckiest guy in the world right now."

Every year I tried to bring this message to life for my students by taking them to Washington, DC. I've led two student trips to Israel and six trips to Europe. The chaperones who assisted agree on the importance of building a sense of wanderlust in our youth. During each excursion, I loved to ask the students to reflect on their day. Some of their most enthusiastic answers involved their "free time" when they were exploring on their own.

One of the ways we find our happiness is by exploring new worlds. We need to get off the sofa, shut off the screen du jour and all the techno-traps that rob us of our individuality, open the front door, and just take off to seek your riches, your purpose, your destiny.

I have a great cartoon above my desk in which Christopher Columbus is sitting on the couch, remote control in hand, staring at a television set. The caption reads, "I wonder what is on the Discovery Channel?"

If Columbus were alive today, would he be content sitting in the comfort of his rec room or man-cave clicking through hundreds of cable TV stations? Or would he be wondering what was on the other side of the world?

What if Lewis and Clark had wondered what was on the National Geographic channel rather than wondering what was on the other side of those mountains?

What if my maternal grandparents had awaited the European Nightmare rather than setting sail for the American Dream?

What if Neil Armstrong had only taken one small step rather than that giant leap for mankind?

If they had, would these adventurers have forgone their riches, their purpose, their destiny of opening new worlds for us?

Adventures and experiences await. New worlds remain hidden. Your species is waiting to meet you and see what you can do.

If you could go anywhere in the world, what EXACTLY is preventing you from going there?

What are you waiting for?

For permission? For it to be a safe environment? For it to be hassle-free? For it to be comfortable?

I thought so!

Overcome those obstacles and make that adventure happen.

How interesting you are, depends upon how interested you are!

How interested, and consequently how interesting, are you?

Indeed.

# 7. How do you seek out states of awe-some-ness!

A couple years after my wife and I got back from three months in Alaska, Patti Jo said to me, "It's time for another major adventure."

I thought, *Great! This is the woman I love.*

I replied, "Where to this time? Africa? Israel? The Appalachian Trail?" After I listed about twenty potential adventures, she lovingly said, "All of our friends are having kids. I want to have children too."

When she said this, I imagined an anchor and chain around my leg for the next twenty years.

But then she said those three magic words: "It would be a new experience." (I'm not good at math.)

I immediately said, "Ok, but first, how about we go on a three-week adventure before we 'have a ball and chain'?" Although I may have said "have a child." "Let's do ten days in the wilderness of the Boundary Waters Canoe Area on the Minnesota-Canadian border followed by ten days in the craziness of Manhattan. What an extreme cultural shock!"

I knew this would be hard for her to pass up, and she didn't.

After some planning, we spent ten days canoeing the old border route water trail and portaging in one of the largest wilderness areas in the US. We saw moose, the northern lights, and the milky way. We heard wolves howling and loons calling. We experienced solitude and stillness. For days at a time we would not see another person. I even got seasick canoeing across one of the largest lakes in the BWCA.

Finally, we woke up on our last wilderness morning, sat by a fire while drinking our morning coffee, and listened to the loons without another soul in sight. Then we tore down camp, packed up our gear and paddled out to our car. After driving to Minneapolis, we caught a plane to New York, and by midnight we were surrounded by the sights and sounds of Times Square. A priceless day! A precious day! A perfect day!

Around midnight, we noticed a crowd had gathered. Being naturally curious, we ventured into the crowd, which was watching the making of a film across the street. Al Pacino and Billy Dee Williams, posing as undercover cops, walked out of a strip club and got into an unmarked squad car, and then drove off. The car went around the block and parked in its original space again so another take could be shot.

After numerous takes, it was past one o'clock in the morning. I looked at my wife and said, "This is fun, being with the crowd and all, but let's try and get in the movie!"

I got a nervous look from her that said, "What are you thinking? This isn't something I want to be part of."

I said, "Let's go to the corner, and when they re-do the same scene, the car will go around the block, and I'll jump in front of IT and get hit by two Hollywood stars.

Smiling, she said, "Ok!" Obviously, she was thinking that this mad idea would only endanger me, not her. So away we went, leaving the crowd behind.

We headed to the corner and had a slice of pizza and a beer as we waited. At 2:00 a.m., the car finally approached. Billy Dee Williams drove with Al Pacino in the passenger seat. It had been a long day for them too, and they looked like anyone would when all they want to do is get some sleep but the director kept saying, "Just one more take."

The light turned red and I headed over to the driver's-side window of the stopped car. With the dumbest, most obnoxious expression I could muster, I waved my hands frantically while balancing a beer and a slice of pizza.

Pacino saw my bizarre behavior out of the corner of his eye, leaned over, grabbed his gut and let out a huge belly laugh. Billy Dee glanced to his left to see what was so funny—I was about 6 inches from his face, and he was startled. But then he leaned back with a huge grin. Suddenly, the light turned green and they drove off. The entire episode took no more than five seconds. While the crowd around the corner was still waiting for them to show up, I got a belly laugh from two Hollywood stars.

Standing in a crowd is nowhere near as fulfilling—or as fun—as standing out in a crowd.

I used to tell my students that the band members of the Eagles, which happened to be our school mascot, were ex-students of mine. They picked their band name to pay homage to their high school alma mater. After explaining this, I often got quizzical looks—which, by the way, I got a lot of from my students.

My favorite line from the Eagles is, "So often times it happens we live our lives in chains when we never even know we have the key." It is the crowd that chains us and keeps us from reaching our full potential, our uniqueness.

Free yourself from the chains that weigh you down. We are not born with these chains—they accumulate link by link throughout our lives and before we realize it, we have become attached to the iron ball. Get out of your comfort zone—comfort is for those in the dawn of life and those in the dusk of life.

Over the next few years, Patti Jo and I would have two ball-and-chains named Erica and John. What an adventure that was… and continues to be.

When was the last time you felt the chains of the crowd preventing you from doing something you really wanted to do?

Did you eventually break free?

If not, why not?

Actress Helen Hayes, who continued to act into her eighties, once stated, "If you rest, you rust." As Neil Young sang, "Rust Never Sleeps." (Which reminds me of the epitaph on a robot's gravestone: "Rust in Peace." Again, I digress.)

We need to be judged by our determination, not our duration. Wrinkles on our face and the number of years we've lived isn't what ages us—it is the desertion of our enthusiasm, our ideals, and our lost sense of wanderlust.

Major accomplishments, achievements, and awakenings never take place in our comfort zones.

When was the last time you said to yourself, "I cannot believe I am here." Maybe I should have asked, when was the last time you screamed with enthusiasm, "I cannot believe I am here!" Were you ever so awe-struck that you didn't want to leave a place? Have you ever paused and thought, *This is wonderful, sublime, awesome, or simply perfect?*

As I had my morning coffee in the Boundary Waters Canoe Area, that was a moment when I had those feelings—when I realized that, at that very moment, all was right with the world... and I was one with the world.

I love the BWCA of northern Minnesota. I have gone up there at least once every year since 1978. It was the place my girlfriend, look-ing at me from the front of the canoe, realized she was going to marry me. It was the place I developed the best friendships of my life with my buddies. It was the place we visited with our two kids every year. For both our children, the mantra "You can go with us when you get out of diapers" was a major incentive to becoming potty trained.

I missed going to the Boundary Waters one year—it was 2016—and it killed me intellectually, emotionally and spiritually. It was the year of my campaign for state senate. After that, I promised I would never miss another year in my "Walden."

Last summer, after my wife and I paddled away from our camp-site in the Boundary Waters, we discovered an island about the size of a large truck. We pulled up our canoe, and for three hours we watched a seagull family playing on a rock. I felt as if "All was right with the world." For that brief time, I felt as if my wife and I were the only people in the world. Sublime!

At our fall workshop, one of my colleagues would always ask, "Make it to the Boundary Waters this summer"?

I usually replied, "Of course."

Then he'd ask how it was, and I would say something about it raining every day, or sometimes would tell him that the mosquitoes, carriage flies, no-see-ums, wood ticks, biting black flies, gnats, horse flies, or whatever the bug du jour was, were absolutely the worst ever." Sometimes I'd bring up a malady that had struck us like poison ivy or a stomach bug. He would say, "Horrible, huh?" And I would reply, "No, it was wonderful, best trip ever!"

I'd say that not because I like being miserable, but I like being alive!

Where do you go to recapture your soul?

Where do you go to get re-charged?

Where do you go to get away from it all?

Where do you go to find AWE?

Seek out states of *awe-some-ness*, refuse to be *awe-deprived*!

I am not sure when I had my first transformative moment—that moment when you know you are being transformed by an experience and never want it to end. Those moments can be few and fleeting, but when you experience one, you immediately know it.

Those are moments when you feel so in AWE that perhaps you were moved to tears—or so amazed that you gained an new appreciation for life.

Those are moments in which even the most elegant and poetic words can never describe how you are feeling.

Those are TRANSFORMATIVE MOMENTS—events that have moved us, shaped us, placed us into a better place, moved us forward and outward and upward. The defining characteristic of a transformative moment is the realization that *I never want this to end*. They are events that take our breath away, that make us truly thankful for the opportunity to experience it.

As children we have all had those moments. Riding alongside my grandfather on a Sunday drive to Pattison State Park. Having lunch with my grandmother at the Androy Hotel. My mom singing to me, "You are my sunshine, my only sunshine." My first kiss, on that swing set. A brilliant sunset with friends on a wilderness camping trip. Sitting on a rock with my wife watching turtles laying eggs. That colonoscopy. (Oh, wait!)

Times when you stop and say "I never want this to end!"

Leaving you breathless and speechless, as we pause and say:
THIS IS TOTALLY AWESOME!
THIS IS TOTALLY AMAZING!
THIS IS TOTALLY LIFE CHANGING!
This is a 1000 WOWS!

I have been so very fortunate to have had more than my share of transformative moments. I have listed a Top Ten here.

1. Looking up from the bottom of the Grand Canyon
2. Looking down at the Dead Sea after hiking up to Masada
3. Crossing into East Berlin at the height of the Cold War
4. Taps playing at the Tomb of the Unknown Soldier
5. Entering Auschwitz
6. Walking my daughter down the aisle on her wedding day
7. My teenage son saying, "Thanks for taking me here!" on a wilderness trip
8. Seeing Rembrandt's *Night Watch*
9. Gazing up at the Statue of Liberty
10. Seeing the pile of rubble that once was the Twin Towers

Make a list of your transformative moments. Stop reading now and make a list of your truly transformative moments!

Where did your adventures/investments take you?

What fears did you have to overcome?

When and what was the last major investment you made in yourself?

Did it prove transformative?


As you will see, your list of transformative moments will define who you are.

Moments of personal growth.

Moments that took your breath away.

Moments that perhaps became the Mile-stones and Stepping-stones and Key-stones of your life!

Reflect upon your defining transformative moments and plan some more!

Refuse to be *awe-deprived*!

As a teacher, I love telling the stories of explorers, settlers and wanderers—those who refused to sit still and become American Idles, and those who had hoped to become American Idols.

Maybe what we need today is another JFK to challenge the next generation.

When JFK said we will send a man to the moon, was it really a call to wander?

When JFK established the Peace Corps, was it really a call to wander?

When JFK named his programs the New Frontier, was it really a call to wander?

I wonder.

How do you seek out states of *Awe-Some-Ness*?

That is awesome!

# 8. How have your misfortunes added fortune to your life?

Misfortune builds character, and your character is the greatest of fortunes.

By trying to find my Walden, I have faced some harrowing wilderness experiences.

My wife and I love the solitude and seclusion of our BWCA wilderness trips. One year we were camping there with another couple and their dog. We had gone on a day trip, but our friends had accidentally left their dog food out. When we came back, a huge bear had already devoured the dog food and was looking for more. We scared him away, hung our food bags from a tree, and had a peaceful time around our campfire.

In the middle of the night, I heard our food bags crash to the ground. Then I heard a bear ripping them apart. I was terrified as I climbed out of my tent into the dark night and started yelling to no avail. The bear, which had already scored food at our camp, was not about to leave until he had finished eating everything we had.

Suddenly, I heard my friend shout, "I have a gun, and I'm going to fire it." A second later a gunshot echoed for miles throughout the lake country and the frightened bear scampered away. Patti and I were shaking and concerned that we barely had enough food to last for the rest of the trip. We didn't sleep well that night knowing a huge bear was out there somewhere. I not only learned a valuable lesson about food storage in the woods, but I got this story to tell as well.

One summer, while backpacking on the Superior Hiking Trail, the temperature spiked to over 90 degrees and Patti Jo and I had run out of water. We finally came upon a swamp with putrid water, but water nevertheless. I filled my thermos and added two iodine tablets, then drank up. Ten days later, I was on a wilderness canoe trip, when the nasty signs of giardia kicked in. Giardia is a parasite from beaver feces that takes effect about ten days after ingesting it. When I got sick, I immediately knew why.

Back in civilization, a doctor gave me a prescription that made me feel much better. The next day, though, I was in so much pain I couldn't sit up. My wife took me to the emergency room, and they took an X-ray of my belly. As my wife and I awaited the results, nurses started looking at pointing and laughing at somebody's images. Neither the nurses or my wife and I knew the images were mine. Suddenly, a doctor entered, grabbed the images and sat down next to me.

"No one in the office has ever seen a gas blockage this large," he explained. "The prescription you've been taking was for a person two hundred pounds larger than you, and the result is you're producing a lot of gas."

A nurse gave me an injection of something they said would help, I farted for over an hour, a steady stream of flatulence. My wife drove home with the windows down. I learned a valuable lesson about untreated water, and I got this story to tell as well.

For a year I had been planning a ten-day kayaking trip with a buddy around Isle Royale, the largest island in Lake Superior. Less than a hundred people circumambulate the island every year. Unfortunately, before leaving I broke my ankle. I decided, however, that I was not going to cancel this adventure. After all, I'd be sitting in a kayak—what would I need my ankle for?

On our first kayaking day, we were rounding a point on the island when we hit a riptide and both of us were thrown into the lake. The waves crashed us into the rocks. I couldn't use my one good leg to gain a foothold, so I just hung onto the kayak using my good leg to kick to shore. I was rising and falling with each wave, and I grew afraid that if my healing leg crashed into one of the huge boulders beneath the surface I'd re-break my ankle. Finally, we made it to shore and spent the night recovering our gear, drying out, trying to stay warm, and anticipating what the next day might bring. I learned a valuable lesson about riptides, and I got this story to tell as well.

The most daunting incident I experienced was with a group of University of Wisconsin students. Our tent ripped wide open on the last night of a week-long backpacking trip to the Bear Tooth Mountains in Wyoming. We had been driven into the tent at night when a winter storm surprised us—it was August, for goodness sake. Winds blew sleet against the tent walls as the temperature plummeted to around thirty degrees. The tent poles had bent and we were taking turns holding up the sides of the tent when the seam tore open and in seconds the tent was flooded. The tent and all of our stuff was suddenly floating in ice water. Our sleeping bags were soaking wet. Hypothermia dangerously started setting in.

I inexplicably decided that hiking out right then, in the middle of the night, in the mountains eight miles from our bus, was the best idea ever. If I had tried to do this, I would have certainly died. One of the group leaders from another tent realized I was going into hypothermia. He got his stove lit, boiled some water, put three packs of hot chocolate and a stick of butter into a mug, and told me to drink up.

In my muddled state, I yelled, "I do not eat butter! I hate butter! I've never put it on toast, popcorn, baked potatoes or pancakes. Never, on anything! I hate butter, and I will not be eating a stick of it. I don't care if I die on this mountain!" I felt like Dr. Seuss's Joey being told by Sam-I-Am to "Try it, try it, you will see."

After I calmed down, I drank the concoction and liked it. I crawled into my wet sleeping bag and let that drink do its magic. Within minutes, I was warm and my body heat started drying the inside of my sleeping bag. In the morning, I emerged alive. I had learned a valuable lesson about butter, and I got this story to tell as well..

Occasionally in class, I would mention these lessons to my students. "You need to have hassles, hurdles, and hindrances, in order to become bigger, brighter and better!" I'd tell them.

Remember that there are many ways to fail, but never taking a chance is the greatest failure of all.

Dare to Fail! Your destiny is not a matter of chance. It is a matter of choice.

Imagine if the boy candle never asked the girl candle to go out with him. When he did, she said yes, and they were delighted. But I digress.

Winston Churchill wrote, "Success is going from failure to failure without loss of enthusiasm."

We are all products of our experiences, and if you look hard enough and are willing to fail, there is always a new experience to be found.

The twists and turns,
The trials and tribulations,
The tragedies and turmoil,
The disasters and disappointments,
All these make us stronger and wiser.

When I was in grade school, I wanted to be a magician. All my friends said it was a stupid idea and I would absolutely suck at it. Ignoring them, at a school variety show, I performed my magic act and made the entire audience disappear. But at least I tried.

In middle school, I wanted to be in the speech club because I was certain that I could deliver a great speech. All my friends said it was a stupid idea and that I would suck at it. At my first speech tournament, by all accounts, I gave a very moving speech. The entire audience moved out into the hall. But at least I tried.

In high school, I wanted to enter a pun contest sponsored by the school paper. All my friends said it was a stupid idea and I would suck at it. I submitted ten puns, hoping one of them would win. No pun-in-ten did. But at least I tried.

In college, I wanted to open up a restaurant on the moon. All my friends said it was a stupid idea and I would totally suck at it. To prove them wrong, I opened a restaurant on the moon. Critics loved the food, but I went out of business after just one week. Evidently it lacked atmosphere. But at least I tried.

After college, I decided to open a charter school. All my friends said it was a stupid idea and that I would suck at it. So I opened up a school for Cyclops. It was not very successful—I only had one pupil. But at least I tried.

But, I digress.

If I had listened to my friends, I would not be the person I am right now.

Sometimes in life, the feces hits the fan!—in a big way—covering one in quite a mess. This can be quite discouraging. However, as the settlers of the American frontiers and the soldiers of the American battles knew, sometimes when the feces hits the fan, it is our reaction that will determine our ability to overcome the mess.

So, stop asking:
What if I fail?
What if I flounder?
What if I fall?
What if the feces hits the fan?

And simply ask:
What if?
When did you last dare to fail?
Which of your misfortunes gave you the greatest wealth?
If you could go back and change one mistake, what would it be?
When did you last take a great chance and failed, and yet discovered it was all worthwhile?
What fear or apprehension has kept you from moving forward, or moving outward, or moving upward?
How have your misfortunes added fortune to your life?

# 9. Are you having the best day ever?

It was a perfect summer, the 'best ever!'" During back-to-school workshops, when people ask me how my summer was, I usually reply, "It was the best ever!" I'm often accused of overusing the phrase, "best ever." But in truth, every summer has always been better than the previous one. In the current summer I did not repeat the mistakes I had made in the past, and I had all kinds of new experiences.

I recently met a man about my age who asked me how my summer was.

I replied, "It was the best ever!"

"Wow," he said. "I haven't had a best summer since I was eight years old."

We cracked up.

Friends and acquaintances often ask "How was your day?" or "How was your weekend?" or "How was your summer?" My reply is almost always, "It was the best ever!"

Self-reflection may cause one to say that I have a Be-Attitude about life—the word "beatitudes" is derived from the Latin "beatus" or beautiful. Be in the moment!

For thousands of years, prophets, poets, playwrights and philosophers have pondered questions about human existence. Some of the deepest philosophical of questions are:

What is human nature?
What are inalienable rights?

Is there a God?

Why am I here?

Beatles or Stones?

Where is the nearest bathroom?

Yet among the questions that have never been answered is:
What is the meaning of life?

The reason so many have failed to answer that question is because the answer is different for each of us. It's different for every human being because every human being is different. The answer is different at different stages and settings of our lives. We are constantly evolving and redefining our purpose. I believe it is more important to ask: "Do I have meaning in this moment? Is there a purpose to this day?"

I begin every day of my life with these three questions:

Who am I going to reach out to today?

What am I going to enjoy about today?

How am I going to grow today?

While lying in bed, standing in the shower or sitting at my desk, I reflect on those three questions every morning—EVERY SINGLE DAY! The answer to those three questions becomes my mission statement for that day.

It was not long after my car accident over forty years ago that I began asking myself these three thought-provoking questions every morning. It was my affirmation, my pronouncement, that I had been given another day—so, what am I going to make of it?

At the end of every day, I pause and reflect on those same three questions, then give myself a grade for the day. I guess that's the teacher in me. Some days I am so proud of how I answered those three questions that I award myself an "A."

## Question One: Who am I going to reach out to today?

Reach out!

Reconnect!

Do you know anyone who may need you today? Will you be

there for them? Who is depending on you for something, somewhere, sometime today? Who may not even realize they are depending on you for something, somewhere, sometime today? Who will appreciate a few thoughtful words, a nice gesture, a random act of kindness? Which member of our species could use a solid hug or a sincere smile? Who may breathe a little bit easier today because of you? Who are you going to reach out to today? To leave one human happier because of you is a gift to all of humanity. It could be a phone call, a hand-written note, a word of kindness, or simply telling someone, "I am glad I know you," or "It is great to see you," or "It is so great to hear your voice."

Try it. Not only will the recipient benefit from your kindness, but you will too. Be a hero to someone, somewhere, somehow today. The only thing more impressive than our actions are the resulting chain reactions. Make a plan.

## Question Two: What am I going to enjoy about today?

Reach in!

Rejoice!

Enjoy today.

So many of us say there will be other days to enjoy, but what if this was the only day left? If you cannot think of anything you are going to enjoy about today, you need to think harder. Life is too full of wonderful moments and meanings and memories. Get out there and start growing.

If I do not plan to enjoy part of my day, at the end of it I may realize I never smiled or laughed. An entire day went by without a feeling of *joie de vrie*. Granted, nothing beats a hearty, spontaneous laugh or a smile brought on by a surprise. But nonetheless, what will bring you joy on this day? Every morning, I need to ask myself what I am looking forward to today that will bring me happiness and pleasure and joy? The price of a smile is the same as a frown. The only thing more impressive than our actions are the resulting chain reactions. Make a plan!

## Question Three: How am I going to grow today?

Reach Up!

Revitalize!

What I do today is important. I am exchanging a day of my life for it. Time without change produces only age. How interesting you are is dependent upon how interested you are. Be interested. Be interesting.

Strive every day to be wiser at the end of the day than you were when you woke up. New adventures, new experiences, and new territories are awaiting you. If you cannot decide between two activities, always choose the one you have never done.

Be curious! As I have said repeatedly throughout this book, a day without growth is a wasted day. Remember, you may not always be doing the right thing, but you must always be doing something! Take a look at your list of Undertakings Before the Undertaker. Which items on your list can you do today? The only thing more impressive than our actions are the resulting chain reactions. Make a plan!

What is your purpose today?

Refuse to be bored!

This has been my modus operandi, my mission in life, my so-called mission statement. Sometimes, of course, my daily mission goes awry, usually on days when spontaneity surprises me.

Walking through the school's resource center one semester, I greeted the same three students who were working before school. I always greeted them with words of encouragement, or a pearl of wisdom, or a joke. One day I was just pontificating when I blurted out, "Be appreciative, be humorous, and be adventurous today."

As soon as I uttered those words, I knew they meant more to me than to them. Those three words—appreciate, humorous, adventurous—had just come out in a stream of consciousness. I wondered, *Did I just come up with the three best words for people to live by?*

When we ask people how they are and they mechanically respond, "Not bad," or "Could be worse," or "I'm still above ground," I have to wonder—when did we set the bar so low?

I have never liked the farewell statement, "Have a nice day." It seems hollow, empty, overdone and insincere. So, how could we improve upon this national salutation? How about this:

Be Appreciative

Be Humorous

Be Adventurous

This provides an "AHA" moment. Every day we should strive for a moment of surprise, triumph or pleasure. As I often say, "A day without an epiphany is like a day without an exclamation point! We should seek out "AHA" moments. Those times when we are at peace, when we achieve clarity, when we are at one, and when we have a sudden realization that it all makes perfect sense. We should have as many "AHA" moments as we can every day.

If we have truly evolved, where will the evolution process eventually take us? What is our final destination? What is the perfect day? Look how far we have advanced in just a few hundred years. What if every day of our lives we strive to be Appreciative, Humorous, and Adventurous? AHA! When we part company, what if we said to one another "Have an AHA day."

May you be Appreciative. May you be Humorous. May you be Adventurous. May you have an AHA! day.

Appreciative: One who is lively, active, vigorous, and spirited about others.

Humorous: One who uses laughter and smiles to bring about joy.

Adventurous: One who undertakes risk, takes a chance, seeks out daring enterprises.

AHA!

Those three words are my mission statement.

My three questions are:

1. Appreciative—Who am I going to reach out to today?
2. Humorous—What am I going to enjoy about today?
3. Adventurous—How am I going to grow today?

Think about the perfect person, the perfect day, the perfect life—a life in which you showed appreciation, were humorous and sought out adventure. Think about it. That would really be something.

So, right now:

Pause and think about the last time you made a difference in some one's life.

Pause and think about the last time you felt great about your life.

Pause and think about the last time you took a chance to improve your life.

52

I had a sign above my classroom door that said, "How interesting you are depends upon how interested you are." For those that are interested, life will be interesting. I'd often ask my students, "How interested are you today?"

Are you waiting for others to entertain and enrich you?

Think about the most interesting people you know. What makes them so interesting? Why did you pick them? Probably because they are interested in filling every day of their lives with as many new and varied experiences as possible.

Begin one day—today perhaps—by asking yourself these three questions:

Who am I going to reach out to today?

What am I going to enjoy about today?

How am I going to grow today?

This becomes your mission for the day! An AHA! day

Then, at the end of the day, give yourself a grade.

What is your daily mission statement?

What is your purpose for today?

Who are you going to reach out to today?

What are you going to enjoy about today?

How are you going to grow today?

How successful were you on your mission today?

What grade did you award yourself?

Have the best moment, the best hour, the best day, the best week, the best month, the best season, the best year, the best decade—simply the best life ever with whatever time you were given.

What is keeping you from having the best day ever today?

Are you having the best day ever?

# 10. Does your matter, matter?

The greatest compliment I can pay you is, "You are a character." You are unique and exceptional. You are far from ordinary. There is no one in the world quite like you. According to anthropologists, over 80,000,000,000 people have lived on planet earth, and yet there never has been—and never will be—another you. You are literally one in eighty billion. On the very day you were born, they broke your DNA mold. Over my teaching career, I have taught twelve thousand students, none of them remotely alike.

Your uniqueness is irreplaceable! Where would we be if not for you? Who would fill the void in your absence? NO ONE!

You are more than just molecules, muscles and matter. Your uniqueness matters!

Once, at a school conference, a mother told me that her daughter was having a hard time fitting in at school, and that she was not a typical student. I told her, "It would be a tragedy if everyone was like your daughter."

The mother looked at me with a quizzical expression that seemed to say, "Have you been listening to me, and did you say what I thought you just said?"

After a few seconds of uncomfortable silence, I added, "And it would be a tragedy if there was no one like your daughter."

She smiled warmly and nodded her agreement. We must all march to the beat of our own drummer.

Your uniqueness is irreplaceable. Without you, the world would be a much different place—a much smaller place. In fact, we may not even recognize the world, it may be unrecognizable to us, had you not played your part.

Your face, your fingerprints, your DNA—these are your physical attributes. Below the material surface, however, lies your idiosyncrasies, your personality, your traits, your soul. These things are what make you a character, a one-and-only you. Your character is the greatest of fortunes, the divine spark that ended up as you. A huge void would exist in the cosmos if your soul was not there to fill that space. That space we call you.

What was the first creature to crawl out of the stagnant mire with a conscience? With a soul? With a spirit?

When could that creation reflect on the meaning of their life? When could that beast wonder, "Why am I here?" When did that animal first think, "How can I help further evolve my species?"

What is this thing that philosophers have been wondering about for thousands of years?

When did we humans first ask these eternal and existential questions rather than merely surviving for another day?

There is so much more to our existence than merely existing.

I used to tell my classes that I was going to bring a giant blender into the room. Then I'd point at a random student and say, "I'm going to put you into that blender and hit puree until all that is left of you is pure liquid. Then I'll pour you onto the floor."

After this, I'd say, "Next, I'm going to puree a penguin into pure liquid and pour it out next to you. What would be the difference between these two liquids? Are we humans merely carbon, hydrogen, oxygen, and nitrogen plus a few trace minerals and elements—just like the penguin. Or are we humans something more? Is there something more to our existence? What are we really made of?"

Scientists tell us that all the chemicals and elements in our bodies are worth a few hundred dollars, so I would challenge my students by asking, "What are you worth?" Is a few hundred dollars what you were thinking?"

Really, what is your life worth financially?

What is your value to your family? Your friends? Your community? Humanity?

How many lives will you touch by inspiring them, encouraging them, making them laugh or smile?

After 9/11, the government decided to compensate the families of the victims. They had to decide what each person's life was worth. Was it based on their current salaries multiplied by the number of years of work they had left? Is that their true worth? Or is there something more to existence than salary?

I liked to tell my students that taxpayers have spent over a hundred thousand dollars on each one of them since they entered kindergarten. "Think about it!" I'd say to them. "How is our investment in you working out? When you walk across that stage at your graduation, what will those in attendance say about you? I hope they will say, 'She was worth spending all that money on,' or 'He was a really good investment.'"

You are more than just molecules, muscles and matter!

You are a creation of the highest intelligence.

You are more than just molecules, muscles and matter.

What are you truly made of?

I am not sure if this story is a myth or if it actually happened, but it really doesn't matter. After the Japanese attacked Pearl Harbor and destroyed the 7th Fleet, which brought the isolationist USA into the global conflict, US Lieutenant Doolittle wanted to act immediately. An attack on Japan, he said, must be swift and certain. Japan had awakened a sleeping giant! Yet at this point in the war, any attack on Japan would be a suicide mission. The pilots and the bombardiers would probably never make it back home.

Doolittle lined up his bombing crews. He told them they might not make it back alive, explaining that any one of them could take one step back to signal they did not want to go on the mission. "No one will judge you," he said.

No one stepped back. Doolittle approached a service member who looked like a high school student. He said to the young man, "Son aren't you afraid of dying?"

The young man replied, "Sir, I am more afraid of not mattering!"

Make your matter matter!

Have you mattered?

Do you matter?

Will you matter?

Will you make a difference? Where will your influence end?

What is your purpose in being here?

Why were you born? Who are you? Why are you here?

Have you earned this?

Who thinks the world of you?

Who believes that you are the greatest?"

I once had a poster ranking the top one hundred films ranked by the American Film Institute (AFI). It was prominently displayed on my classroom wall, and I referred to it regularly. Whenever I could turn my students on to an underappreciated art form I would. I loved my film nights at which I would show a few of my favorite films. They may not have been curriculum-related, but I could usually make them fit in somehow to expose my students to films that did not contain any explosions, gunshots, sex scenes or action heroes. Many of my students had never seen a foreign or silent film before my class. I showed *Citizen Kane, City Lights, Life is Beautiful, Saving Private Ryan* and *Harold and Maude.*

*Citizen Kane* is number one on the AFI film list. One evening I had over eighty sophomores show up to my film night. I had really built up *Citizen Kane* as a masterpiece of filmmaking. I was nervous, though, that the students would not "understand" the film. That they would be too young, too immature, too shallow to follow the film's artistry, intent and purpose. When the movie ended, they all applauded. I got very emotional and felt proud of these fine young people.

*Harold and Maude* is about a young man searching for meaning in his life. The soundtrack by Cat Stevens is brilliant. The last week of my teaching career, the choir—many of the singers were in my class and had seen the film—came down the hall toward my room singing Cat Stevens lyrics:

If you want to sing out sing out,
and if you want to be free be free!
Cause there's a million things to be,
You know that there are…

When one moves forward and outward and upward, do we not *all* move forward and outward and upward? Look at the list of one hundred films on the AFI list. How many have you seen? Make it a goal to see them all in the next few years. Add that goal to your "Undertakings before the Undertaker" list. Next time you and your friends want to watch a movie, suggest one from the AFI list. Tell your friends you want to be a littler "richer and wiser" after investing two hours of your life on something. Give it a try, You may be surprised. They may even applaud!

Many of these films are about one person overcoming odds and making an impact on the world that will be felt long after they are gone. What they have in common is the message that one person can make a difference, and with a lot of courage and passion every person can improve upon a near perfect universe.

I came of age watching American films of the 1970s—pure escapism. Comedies and action films dominated that era. I was in my mid-twenties when a local art film cinema was showing a retrospective on Charlie Chaplin. I told Patti, "I have never seen a silent film before. Let's go see a Chaplin movie." I was in love instantly with the *Little Tramp*. We ended up going to see three more Chaplin films during the series, and I fell more in love with Chaplin with each viewing.

Chaplin's Little Tramp was "Everyman." He represented all of us at some point in our lives. The Little Tramp taught me to listen with my eyes—it was a silent film, after all. He taught me that actions speak louder than words. Chaplin's masterpieces truly were the work of a genius. He was director, actor, producer, writer, editor and composer, taking five years in some cases to finish a film. I ended up showing *City Lights* and *Modern Times* at my film nights. Usually, his films got the loudest applause because the students knew they were seeing something special. The last shot in *City Lights* may be the greatest ending in film history. I cannot describe it—you just have to see it.

You are a creation of the highest intelligence. Each and every one of you will impact this world—this universe. What that impact will be is up to you. You have the opportunity to:

Know one life has breathed easier because of you.

Know one heart has beaten a little louder because of you.

Know one child has been enriched because of you.

Know one event was a little sweeter because of you

That it is indeed "a wonderful life"—that your matter did indeed matter. That the little bit of divine spark that found its way into you did indeed matter. That you understand your purpose on this planet is to leave it grander than you found it—to improve upon a near-perfect universe.

Arguably, the greatest holiday film—maybe the greatest film ever—is *It's A Wonderful Life*. As a young adult, it was the first life-changing film I ever saw. It's about an individual seeking meaning in his life. I saw it when I was about twenty-one. I cried like a baby, and I still cry every time I see it, sometimes during the opening credits. As the film progresses, without giving anything away, George Bailey wishes he had never been born because his life was not meritorious, momentous, or memorable. He believed he was broke, both financially and as a man. He was discouraged and needed help to see the light.

We all do at times. At times that light is right before our eyes; at other times it is hidden from view. Yet it is always there—we just need to open our eyes to see that light.

In the movie, an angel grants George Bailey his wish that he had never been born and takes him on a tour of his hometown. Everywhere the angel takes George, nothing and nobody looks familiar. George is bewildered. The angel keeps reminding him that he had not been born, so the town's and resident's existence is very different because of his absence—in many cases much worse. The angel tells George Bailey, "Each person's life touches so many others." George eventually realizes that his life matters.

In the last scene (spoiler alert), the main character opens a book that says, "No man is a failure who has friends." How true! George Bailey, who had considered himself a failure, was indeed the "richest man in town" because he always worked on his friendships.

Who is the richest person you know?

What do you think the world would look like if you had never been born?

Where would your acquaintances, your friends, and your family be without your influence?

Who are your oldest friends? Who are your newest friends? What is a "friend"?

Where would the world be without you?

Who would fill the void in your absence?

After I saw *It's a Wonderful Life* for the first time, I started thinking about all of those forces that, acting independently and interdependently, had saved my eye, my leg, in fact, saved my life. After my accident, I was dependent upon so many nurses, technicians and doctors. Lying on my back for a month, in that hospital bed at seventeen, I began to reflect on all of this. I started to understand the importance of every person I met, and the influence that we mutually have on each other. I began to think about the chain reactions each of us starts with every action we take, and how directly as well as indirectly each human being can ultimately impact thousands of other human beings. I thought about all those forces acting moving us all forward, outward, and upward.

Where will your influence end?

What are you really made of?

These are the questions so many great films ask of us.

It is easy to reflect on when our influence began. It began with your mother saying the words, "I think I'm pregnant." The more intriguing question, though, is where does our influence end? We know it is inevitable and inescapable, unavoidable and unstoppable. Trust me! Our influence on this planet is a given, but how large or small it may be is up to you. Will your influence be immeasurable?

From before you were born until long after you are gone, your presence is felt on earth. Your influence knows no ends. Your life is like a pebble thrown into a pond, leaving ripples going out in every direction. What kind of pebble will you be? A tiny one or a boulder?

Will you be a little ripple or a tsunami for change?

Do you know who jumped off the cliff first—the small pebble or the penguin? The pebble… it was a little boulder. But I digress again.

I have often asked my classes, "Where will your influence end?"

One time in class, I was ranting about all of this when a student raised his hand and said, "My mom is a lunch line lady. Do you really believe she is making a difference, plopping food onto the trays of little kids? A monkey could do that job."

I wanted to tell that kid he should be ashamed of himself, but instead, I paraphrased what Martin Luther King once said:

If a man is called to be a street sweeper,
He should sweep streets as Michelangelo painted,
Or Beethoven composed music,
Or Shakespeare wrote poetry.

He should sweep streets so well that when he comes to die, all the hosts in heaven and earth pause to say: "Here lived a great street sweeper, who did his job well."

Every time I came to the words "he" or "his" or "street sweeper," I changed it to "she" or "her" or "lunch line lady."

That was one of those moments when, as a teacher, I hit a homerun! The right thought, at the right moment, where thirty students all go WOW! A major epiphany!

Where does our influence end?

Our influence knows no boundaries! It is timeless!

Whenever I asked a class of seniors, "What question are you guys sick of?" They usually yell out, "Where are you going to college?" I always preferred to ask *why* are you going to college? I always found this to cause deeper reflection. Whenever I would ask a student in the spring of their senior year, "What are your plans for next year?" and their head would bow. I'd know immediately that they were about to say, "I'm just going to vo-tech," or "I'm just going to community college," their heads lowered in shame.

Boy, did that make me angry. I'd go on a tirade about holding your head up high, being proud of yourself because everyone has a different path. I'd go on and on about why we create that unjust stigma

61

as if not going to a four-year college was a disgrace. Shame on us!

When students, contemplating their post-secondary options, would ask me, "What do you think I should do?" I'd always tell them, "Have fun and don't be ordinary!"

For readers of this book, I add this: Maybe, just maybe, give a little too, sacrifice a little, contribute a part of yourself for the common good.

By now, you may be wondering if I ever taught any of the official content or state-mandated curriculum. That may be my next book.

Our matter does, in fact, very much matter!

# 11. What do you bring to the buffet?

I had a huge banner on my classroom wall that read, "I do not want to spoon-feed you, I want to create a buffet at which you can feast."

When I read the quote to my students, I always added: "And, of course, what do you bring to the buffet?"

Is what you bring to the buffet worth having?

On most days at school, I held up the morning paper at the beginning of every class and began a discussion of the day's events. I was always able to find a hook or a story line relating to the curriculum. Rarely was there a day with no news that I could use to begin class.

On one slow news day, I came into class excited, yelling and screaming with all sorts of body language wildly proclaiming, "They discovered life on the moon." I held up the paper describing that it was a little brown bug about the size of a pinhead with eight legs. I said that they are going to call it a "lunatic," pronouncing it lunar-tick. Then I apologized, saying, "Ok, I made that up. But for real, they discovered life on Mars. It's a white animal about the size of a large piece of fluffy candy. They're going to call it a martian-mellow."

By this point, my enthusiasm was waning and the class was disappointed that they really did not discover life on another planet. So, I told them that they needed to go home tonight because ABC had exclusive video of a nine-foot-tall beast covered in fur that walks upright and lives in the Himalayas. They'd be premiering the video tonight. The newspaper went on and on to say that the video shows the beast doing a thousand sit-ups. They were calling it the "Abdomen-able Snowman!" But I digress.

A student came back the next day disappointed, saying, "There was nothing on the news last night about discovering Yeti." Go figure.

My classroom was covered with signs, posters, newspapers and photos of our nation's history, both past and present. Mobiles, flags, and magazine covers hung from the ceiling. I had a lot of banners in my room. One, from the rotunda of the Jefferson Memorial, stated: "I pledge eternal hostility over every form of tyranny over the minds of man."

One year, as students were taking their finals, I left the room to go bother the teacher next door. When I came back, someone had slightly covered the word "man" with a sign stating "humanity." They had left the word "man" slightly visible behind the new word "humanity." I am sure the student and the class thought I would not notice the change until they all had departed. I noticed it immediately.

I yelled, "Who put that up here? Who thought they could vandalize my room? Who dared to change Jefferson's quote by making some kind of feminist statement?" A girl who had not said a word all term raised her hand and boldly announced, "I was bugged all term by that word MAN and decided to replace it with HUMANITY." Her act of defiance remained up in my room for the rest of my teaching career.

One Monday, I was lecturing when I noticed a student with an anarchy symbol on his folder. I grabbed it and tossed it in the garbage. He yelled at me, and I shrugged my shoulders with a "deal with it" expression. He shouted something and stormed out the room, screaming, "I'm going to the principal."

After he walked out, I plucked the folder out of the garbage and showed the class what I had tossed. The folder had the anarchy symbol scrawled on it. A few students knowingly cracked up. I said, "Wait. The phone is going to ring and it's going to be the principal."

Within minutes the phone rang. It was the assistant principal who said, "Steve, there is someone in my office who is saying you threw his materials in the garbage in front of the class." I thought, *You cannot teach this stuff*. I told the principal I would be down to his office in a few minutes. I then pointed out to the class, some of whom had no idea what was going on, that the young man professed anarchy, meaning no government/no rules, but at the moment he had a grievance he headed off to "The Man"!

As everyone was laughing, the bell rang, and I headed to the office. I walked in, displaying the anarchy symbol on the folder. The student cracked up. "Good one, Cwod," he said before we shook hands. I'm glad he was mature enough to catch the irony.

In class the next day, we discussed tyranny vs. anarchy. I told the class, "When law ends, anarchy begins. Yet Aristotle taught 'When law ends, tyranny begins.'" It was one of those priceless teachable moments. I kept the anarchy-branded folder on my wall for the rest of my career.

I kept my podium full of beanie babies. Every time a student made a brilliant insight or observation, I would throw them a Bald Eagle beanie baby and exclaim, "Student of the Day!" I had a few other beanie babies in the podium. Sometimes I gave out three or four in an hour. I recently got an email from a former student who had graduated fifteen years ago. She told me that she and her brother, another ex-student, reward each other when they ask a good question by proclaiming "Student of the Day."

Sometimes after a really good comment or question, I'd proclaim, "Student of the Millennium."

I had shrines to US Senator Wellstone and the victims and heroes of 9/11. Globes hung from the ceiling, banners and posters plastered the walls and ceilings, and even a Beatle poster or two could be found in my classroom. I had a photo from the opening night of *Citizen Kane*. Hundreds of newspaper front pages and *Time* magazine covers adorned the walls. Also on display were hanging chads from Florida's presidential election of 2000 sent to me by an ex-student. While in my class, she had been an election judge, and a few years later continued her civic duty as an election judge in Florida. Dangling from the ceiling was an empty plastic box that I would point to when I'd accuse students of being "stuck inside the box." And there was more—photos and T-shirts of my thirty student trips to DC, Europe and Israel, and a wide assortment of stuffed animals, toys, trinkets and posters that students had given me during my teaching career.

The year *Toy Story 2* came out, I went gaga over Jessie. I loved her character. By the end of that term, I had six Jessie dolls in my classroom, all of which I still have. Students can be so giving and thoughtful. I talked a lot in class about Jessie's Excitement and Elation and Enthusiasm and Exuberance for Everything.

American Flags hung in every direction, including one that had been flown from our Nation's Capital in my honor and had been presented to me by a congressman. Whenever we stood in class to do the Pledge of Allegiance, students never knew which flag they should face among the dozens on display. The one we did face as we recited the pledge, however, with hands over hearts, was the flag flown from our nation's capital.

That flag I proudly hang in my senate office in St. Paul.

The props I proudly used every single day were reproductions of the Declaration of Independence, the US Constitution and the Bill of Rights. Whenever I would point to the Declaration, I'd tell the class that my friend Nicholas Cage had given me that original copy, and I have no idea how he got it. A few students would get the cultural reference to a popular Cage movie.

Every day I'd refer to what my students simply called "Those five pieces of paper." Every day I'd hold up the morning newspaper and point out a section or article from the Constitution. This is how I began every class. Sometimes I even wore a T-shirt that stated, "The Constitution–I read it for the Articles."

My room contained dozens of signs. Many of my posters, all made by students over the years, presented my favorite quotes. Front and center was a quote by Socrates—"Question Everything"—which I emphasized repeatedly every hour before asking, "Are there any QUESTIONS?"

I may have been the only teacher who, after getting a really stupid question, would tell the questioner, "That is a really stupid question." Students at first would be shocked—they had drunk the 'There is no such thing as a stupid question' Kool-Aid. Hanging next to the

Socrates "Question Everything" banner was one that proclaimed, "He who asks a question is a fool for five minutes. He who does not ask a question remains a fool forever." Whenever I felt a student's question was stupid, I would tell them it was stupid while pointing to that Chinese proverb. The moral, of course, is never stop asking really stupid questions.

I love art. My room showcased some of my favorite paintings. I had a giant eye painted by Magritte that was always keeping a watchful eye upon us. I had a photo mosaic of *Migrant Mother* by Margaret Bourke-White, which was comprised of hundreds of photos of impoverished Americans during the Great Depression. I had Picasso's *Guernica* hanging alongside Sargent's *Gassed*, which depicts the horrors of WWI soldiers blinded by mustard gas and holding onto each other. *Guernica* abstractly depicts the horrors of the WWII fire-bombing of innocent civilians in Guernica, Spain. These were perhaps the two best paintings ever to put the horrors of war onto canvas.

I had four paintings by Norman Rockwell on display, including his interpretation of the words spoken so eloquently by FDR when he declared that a democracy guarantees every individual:

Freedom of Speech
Freedom of Religion
Freedom from Want
Freedom from Fear

The last Rockwell painting in my room was my favorite. "Freedom from Fear" depicts a father and mother tucking their children into bed. The parents are holding a newspaper with a headline boldly stating, "Bombings Kill" and "Horrors Hit." Every parent's greatest fear is that harm may come to their children. Freedom from fear, indeed!

I had a huge print of the Beatle's *Abbey Road* cover. On each Beatle, I placed an "I Voted" sticker that had been given out on election day. I had a lot of "I Voted" stickers strewn about the room, strategically placed on various prints and posters. One of my all-time favorite photos showed a winding six-hour line of people in South Africa waiting to vote. Blacks had never been allowed to vote. Mandela was on the ballot. Voters had to wait in that line for hours.

Whenever a student complained about our electoral system, I'd discuss that fateful photo.

In my room were many photos and letters from my students linked to many wonderful moments. One photo had fourteen students, who were on a choir trip to DC, standing on the steps of the Supreme Court. Each student was holding up a huge letter. Together the letters spelling out "HI MR CWODZINSKI." I was never sure who came up with that idea, but that act of kindness and gratitude motivated me to take students to DC, which I continued to do for the next twenty years.

Where does your influence end? Indeed.

My classroom was a museum—a monument to civic duty, civic virtue and political efficacy. The walls were plastered, the ceiling was covered, there were reminders to vote and participate and get involved and make a difference. There were props and devices on every level surface. Outside my room, students had painted in the hallway all my favorite quotes. My favorite was, "People will not remember what you say, but they will remember how you made them feel," by Maya Angelou. I think it is an interesting quote that aptly reflected a teacher who lectured all hour.

A huge Christmas ornament hung from the ceiling. It was a photo from the last scene in *It's a Wonderful Life* showing the Bailey family in a group hug. It was a prop I often used when the classroom needed a reminder about what was really important in life—family and friends.

God, I loved teaching!

"The Slide" was a toddler's play slide. On the first day of class, I would remind my seniors of the perils of senior slide, pointing to "The Slide." I'd tell them that if they maintained their GPA, their class rank, the rigor of their class load, and continue to work as hard as they could in school, on the last day they could come to class and take "the slide."

I had this great idea about our school's commencement ceremony. I brought my clever and creative idea up to every principal I ever worked for. What if there was a giant "S" on your diploma that meant you maintained your GPA and your rigor throughout your senior year? This would mean that the student would not have to walk down the three steps from the stage at graduation. They could SLIDE down. The shirt buttons of parents would burst with pride watching their children take the slide, and those graduates that did not earn an "S," because they already had taken a slide—well, their parents would be looking down at their feet in shame. I thought this idea would not only deter "senior slide" but also add a little fun to the pomp and circumstance of graduation.

The principals said it was a bad idea. One even said there could be liability issues.

Seriously?

I never understood the concept of Senior Slide. I love teaching seniors in May and June, even though it took every tool in my toolbox to do it successfully. While a few of my peers complained that their "seniors have checked out, they're done, they don't want to be here," I welcomed the challenge. I used to say that if you can inspire seniors in May, you can inspire anyone. When I taught seniors during the last term, I always ended the course with each student delivering their own commencement speech. Sometimes I laughed, sometimes I cried, but I always got inspired. I called their final assignment/speech: Protestations, Proclamations, Predictions and Poetry.

One year I had my students come to class every day with a homemade name tag that would be placed on their desk. Then, facing me would be their names, prominently and artistically displayed, to better help me learn them. On the backside, facing each student, a quote that would inspire them. They'd look at it and reflect upon its meaning and relevance to them. Every day I'd start class by calling on one student to cite their motivational passage. We then spent a few minutes discussing why the student picked that one, and then we'd discuss it as a class. I only did that for a few years—I don't know why I stopped. Maybe it was the administrator who asked me where this activity was in the course outcomes.

I also did yoga for a couple of years. Halfway through our eighty-six-minute class, I'd have the students stand up and do a standing pose. Eagle pose was their favorite, along with warrior pose. It took just a minute and got some oxygen to our brains. It was like a mini-recess.

I only did that for a few years. Again, I don't know why I stopped. Maybe it was the administrator who asked me if I had been properly trained in leading yoga.

Namaste!

I had a large handmade sign that depicted the Latin phrase *Sapere Aude* (Dare to be Wise.) A student made it for me after we got back from DC. On the trip, she kept telling me, "How great this is," and "How great that was." It was as if she was having an awakening at every opportunity. At one point, when she exclaimed, "This is awesome!" I replied "Sapere Aude." She replied: "What is that?" When I told her it means dare to be wise, she nodded in approval as if saying it had been a long time coming. She made me the sign upon our return.

A lot of stuff! Some may say it was not a classroom, but rather Cwod's Playroom.

What does your playroom/office/man-cave/she-shed say about you and what you value?

If you could display one inspiring quote to motivate you and those that stop by your space, which one would you choose?

On the last day of my career I put everything I wanted to keep to one side, and I let my students take what was left. Many walked out with their arms full. One student gazed at my pile and said, "You're going to have some awesome memory boxes in your house."

Yes, I do!

All of this is what I brought to the buffet. I often wonder what my students thought of my buffet and what they took away from it. I certainly know that many of those students contributed greatly to my buffet.

So, what do you bring to the buffet?

# 12. Do you dare enter the marketplace of ideas?

S apere Aude!
   I had a sign on the outside of my classroom door that read, "The Marketplace of Ideas." It was the first thing I wanted my students to see as they entered my classroom. Upon entering, one would be exposed to a wide variety of ideas, facts and opinions—to consider the other person's point of view. Maybe to have an AHA! moment, or an epiphany, or a hearty laugh. Those were my daily goals for thirty-three years.

   Once, during a post-observation, an administrator asked me, "When did you identify for the class your outcomes and learning targets of the lesson?"

   I told him, "I only have one outcome and learning target, and it's the same every single day."

   He asked, "What is that?"

   "That the students can evaluate their ongoing role as an engaged, informed and active citizen of the United States of America."

   The next day I made a banner and placed it on my classroom wall. Every day thereafter I announced the outcomes and learning targets of the day's lecture as I gestured toward the banner. I believe producing good citizens should be the number one objective of our educational system.

I was at a dinner party about ten years ago. Back then, only young people had smart phones. A small group of us, all in our fifties, were speculating and debating who wrote a certain song from the 1960s. We were having a lively discussion when suddenly a much younger person asked what we were talking about. We explained that we were trying to remember who wrote a song from our youth. Before we could finish explaining, she had her smart phone out and proudly proclaimed the answer. We looked around, all of us thinking the same thing. What was more important here—the quizzing, questioning, lively discussion, banter, and camaraderie… or the correct answer?

I thought about my role as an educator and considered what was more important.

The journey? (The discussion and debate)

or

The destination? (The correct answer)

I am not sure which is more important to learning—I need to give that more thought.

An educational coach once called my classroom a "pedagogical black hole." I took that as an extreme compliment. However, I do not believe it was meant to be one. I wanted my classroom to be like LAXATIVES FOR THE BRAIN! Special ed teachers who had students with ADD—Attention Deficit Disorder—would worry about putting their kids in my classroom. There was just way too much to distract the students. *How wonderful*, I thought.

One year we had a speaker during workshop week who talked about having a "Safe Learning Environment" in our classrooms. I thought, *I want my students to be*:

*Battered and bruised.*

*Pushed and pulled.*

*Tattered and torn.*

*Stirred out of their complacency and shaken from their passivity.*

Safe Learning Environments are for those who want to be left alone and not bothered.

Educators, I believe:

Need to maintain a level of arousal, not anxiety.

72

Need to shout in excitement, not anger.

Need to be exciting, refreshing, enthusiastic, engaging, and amusing.

I spoke, lectured and yelled, but students never fell asleep. It was as though I was cranked all the way up to ten, or even eleven. In fact, the students in the classroom next door sometimes suggested that they should get credit for my class as well. They could hear my entire lecture every day through the walls. They believed they could pass my exams, as well as the exams of the class they were sitting in.

I loved teaching my students almost as much as I loved learning from them.

Students would often accuse me of making their heads hurt. I am not sure if it was from me making them think, or from me yelling all hour at decibel levels heard only at airports and rock concerts.

I miss reading about all the things students would convey to me in their course evaluations. I really enjoyed studying their insights and observations. I would ask approximately ten questions, among them being:

What were your expectations of the course?

Have you grown as a person?

One student wrote: "I expected a boring, stupid class. My expectations were greatly exceeded." I was not quite sure how to take that one.

Since leaving my teaching career, I have been going through emails and cards that I kept from my students and colleagues. I had put all the Thank You correspondence in a box to be read someday for a second time. That time began this year. The thing that bums me out the most is that so many letters and cards from ex-students began with, "I'm sure you don't remember me, but I was…" The head injury I suffered back in my senior year damaged my memory and that really sucks.

Here is some of the stuff I got in all those cards and letters (ex-students, maybe you will see your quote here):

"You have instilled in me a sense of urgency to get on with living."

"Continue to destabilize people."

"Thanks for making me a better person. I hope to do the same someday for someone else."

"You have a gift for getting inside people."

"If I were lying on my death bed and you told me I could live, I would do it."

"You are as much a student as we teenagers are. Your exuberance for learning is more contagious than the Ebola virus."

"Thanks for reminding me that life is no video game—there are no do-overs!"

"I now want to shake the earth."

"Thanks for being a teacher that does not teach what we have to know, but what we need to know."

"When thinking seems almost like a hassle, you make it seem mandatory."

"Thanks to you we are no longer condemned to repeat our history."

"My thirst for wisdom and knowledge is now insatiable."

"My mind keeps changing its mind."

"So, are you a liberal or what?"

"Thanks for inspiring us to live loudly."

"You are without a doubt the most insane teacher I ever had, and I loved every minute of it. NO MORE SOMA FOR ME!"

"You taught me to not just be a human being, but a human doing."

"My parents joke that we have Cwod to blame for everything I have become."

"I will find my issue, I will solve my puzzle, I will never turn down a new experience, I will never follow the crowd, I will march to the beat of my own drummer. Thank you for giving me hope."

"You need to ask for a joke book from Santa."

"No longer do I feel estranged from my government."

"Thank you for bestowing upon me a plethora of epiphanies."

"Thanks for everything, I won't let it go to waste."

"I remember going to your class being deathly afraid my ignorance would be revealed."

"I have become obsessed with self-examination."

"On the first day, I was so scared. By day three, I could not wait for class. Do something that scares you today."

"Every day should be a Commencement Ceremony."

"I never wanted to miss your class, even on senior skip day. I was afraid I might miss something."

"You have made an impact on me larger than Tojo's territorial gains of 1942."

"Everywhere me and my friends go somewhere, we find ourselves asking: What would Cwod do?"

"You sparked an inspiration in me that has become a wildfire."

"I wish I could be like you someday. Actually no, I want to be like me someday. Thanks for teaching me that!"

"We are off to college and need thought-provoking intellectually-stimulating questions to get our synapses going... psss, psss, pssss."

"You kept me up at night. I lose sleep because my head is spinning over things you brought up in class that day."

"I keep hearing your voice saying: Get your synapses firing."

"I will always remember sitting too close to the spit-free zone."

"You have turned my ignorance into interest."

"Every day you came to class bubbling with information that would have exploded if you had to wait a minute longer to teach us, so it seemed."

"I left your class everyday feeling confident that I could stand by my opinion, even if I stood alone."

"After one of your tirades, you screamed, "What do you think?" We stared blankly as though you had asked us to fly."

"Your class is not a course, it is a lifestyle."

"You told us we were God's gift to teachers so often we started to believe it. We walked out of your class a foot taller."

"We are experiencing economic decline, arrogant foreign policy, and foolhardy tax cuts. But I sleep better knowing there is a man frantically waving a pointer at some cryptically-scratched chalk on a blackboard."

"Keep making mistakes. It makes you seem human."

"Before your class, my childhood dreams had been replaced by plans for normalcy and financial stability. Then you came along to revive the dreams that had been long forgotten."

"Your appreciation and perception of life will never be the same once you have seen it through the eyes of Steve Cwodzinski."

For all of you who took time out of your busy lives to share your thoughts with me, thank you. I cherish them.

Here is a small sample of my sayings and catch-phrases from over the years that have become part of my schtick:

See me afterclassbeforeclassafterschoolbeforeschoolorzerohour.
Get the Synapses Firing!
Partake in Giant Mental Leaps! (GMLs)
If I become God of This Planet...
IckyBoodily (though this one I must credit to my wife).
Muy Mal.
Are you taking SOMA?
Entertain a minor Epi or a major Epiphany if you will!
Pick any number... Not that one!
The feces hit the fan!
Get out of your comfort zone and order a sad meal.
It's a "College Level Joke" (if no one laughed at my im-material).
God, I loved teaching.
I still miss the smell of chalk in the morning.

I used to save all my pieces of chalk when they got too small to use. One year, on Valentine's Day, I presented my wife a heart shaped candy box. She enthusiastically opened it up, only to find a bunch of used-up pieces of chalk. When she looked up in disappointment, I declared, "You said you wanted a box of chocolates!" Chalk-olates— little pieces of chalk. But I digress.

The Cwod Experience! Do you dare enter the marketplace of ideas?

# 13. Do you keep an open mind as you keep opening doors?

As a young adult, my male friends wanted to go every weekend down to the lake, play Frisbee, and flirt with girls. Which, I must admit was great fun, but I was seeking out even more to my existence. My "girlfriend" and I were in a Platonic relationship. I could call on her to go see a live performance at the local theatre, a foreign film, or an art exhibit. She seemed to be open for anything, so I was looking to take our relationship to the next level. Platonic was fine, but I wanted to kiss, hold hands, and you know, stuff. I was smitten by her.

One night, my special friend called and asked me if I wanted to do "student rush" at the Guthrie Theatre and see Macbeth. I told her "Great, I have never seen Macbeth. What time do you want to meet?" She said "Let's go out for dinner first. I want to tell you something really important." I was definitely intrigued. We met at a Japanese restaurant, again a new experience. I walked in. She was sitting there looking beautiful. I sat down. We chit chatted. Finally, she said "Steve, I want to tell you something I have never told another living person." I thought to myself, as anyone would, this is going to be juicy. She then proceeded to tell me the words I had been dying to hear. She said "Steve, for the first time in my life I am in love." I was going to jump across the table, grab her, kiss her, and scream out in the restaurant "I love you as well" and "I have felt the same way about you for months now" and "I am so glad you feel the same way I do!" However, I said none of that. I let her continue. Then came the shocker. She said, "I am in love for the first time in my life, and it is with another woman." I was nineteen years old and I did not know any gays or lesbians. It was like a ton of bricks just fell on me. I was devastated. I was shocked. I was paralyzed. She told me, "I do not know how to tell her." I did not hear another word she said for the next five minutes. All I kept thinking was how thankful I was for not making a fool of myself by professing my love for her and assumed she obviously must be in love with me. She then asked me, "How do I tell her?" It was an adult conversation I was not ready for, but I tried and I fumbled my way through it. After all I loved her and wanted her to be happy.

I told this story from my younger days for years to my students. I wanted the gay and lesbian students to know my class was welcoming and inclusive. One year, the second I was done telling this story, one of my student's hands shot up asking, "Where is this in the curriculum?" It was as though she had been trained somewhere to question whenever a teacher brought up anything remotely "favoring gay rights." I told her it wasn't, but it is among my lessons not written in the lesson plan. There were to be a few of those students over my career.

During my first years teaching, there was this teacher that would bring in an ex-student that had come out of the closet after high school. He would talk to her classes about his life as a closeted gay high school student. His message was all about "It is ok to be different and accept people for who they are." Parents went ballistic. "She was promoting a deviant lifestyle, if she does not stop she should be fired!" I defended the teacher and her guest speaker, at a school board hearing. The teacher won. That was over thirty years ago.

For years "my issue", was gay rights for my family, for my friends, for my colleagues, and for my students. I had the following letter published in the local newspaper in 2012:

I have taught American Government to high school students for twenty-seven years. During those years I have been accused by students and parents of promoting "gay rights" in my classroom. I have always proudly admitted that: "Yes I am!" I teach that the Declaration of Independence states that "all men are created equal" and that we have unalienable rights to life, liberty, and the pursuit of happiness" and that we established a Constitution to guarantee "We the people" those basic fundamental human rights. Today I celebrate that the teacher, and leader of the free world, has endorsed gay marriage. That each and every American should be allowed to marry their soul mates. I feel vindicated. On behalf of all my past, present, and future gay students I thank you President Obama.

Three years later, I had the following letter published in the local newspaper when Minnesota voted NO to a constitutional amendment that would have defined marriage as between a man and women.

I have taught American Government to high school students for almost thirty years. During all those years I have often been accused by students and parents of promoting "gay rights" in my classroom. I have always proudly admitted that "yes I am!." I teach that the Declaration of Independence states that "all men are created equal" and that we all have "unalienable rights to life, liberty, and the pursuit of happiness" and that we set up governments "to secure these rights." I teach that the US Constitution states that "We the people" will "guarantee to all" the equal protection of the law. TODAY I celebrate! Minnesota law will finally reflect the basic principles that all us American Government teachers teach, as well as preach. For all of my past, present, and future students who wish to marry their soul mates, "We the people" have spoken. Today let us all rejoice knowing we have again proven to the world that the United States continues to be the beacon for freedom.

On one of the last days of my thirty-three-year career I asked the students what was their favorite front pages were, among the hundreds hanging in my room, from the *Minneapolis Star Tribune*. The number one answer was the banner headline from 2012: "Freedom to Marry." I told my students I may agree.

During my first campaign in 2016, I got an email from an ex-student from 1994. He wrote, "You always kept us on our toes wondering if you were a Republican or a Democrat. At times you even seemed to make a game of it. There was one exception, where you did disclose your position and were adamant about it. It was sexual orientation! This was five years before Ellen DeGeneres, and we all remember how controversial that was. It is remarkable that you did this, and it is even more remarkable that you must have known the difference it made to many of us."

I kept that email.

I was five years old, and my grandparents and my mom were going out. Nancy, my sitter, arrived at the door. I was in love with her and was, of course, planning on marrying her someday. She was standing in the entry way and asked my grandma if she "could have a few friends over." I stood behind Nancy facing my grandma, frantically trying to get her attention and violently shaking my head, "No, I want Nancy all to myself!" My grandma said "Yes, of course you can have your friends over, there are drinks and snacks in the fridge."

I tell people I was an only child, which is not entirely true. I wanted my sitter all to myself. So, I filled our sand box with quick sand. Never saw my siblings after that. But, I digress.

So, Nancy and her three friends were in front of the television. I sat fuming somewhere in the corner. Their attentions were focused on the Ed Sullivan showinstead of me. As Ed Sullivan introduced the next act they started screaming and shrieking like nothing I had ever heard before. The Beatles began singing "Close your eyes and I'll kiss you." I knew I had lost my first girlfriend to these Lads from Liverpool. Not quite sure how Nancy fits into this chapter. Maybe a therapist can figure it out.

I loved pointing out that in 1967 they come out with two masterpieces in one year: "Sgt. Pepper's Lonely Hearts Club Band" and "The Magical Mystery Tour." Then comes one of the most important years in world history: 1968! The world was suffering and in pain. The world was in turmoil as it faced thundering trials and tribulations. The world was looking to The Beatles for a message, a sign, anything to tell us through all the turbulence and troubles of that trying year, what they were thinking. Each month the world waited. Finally in August came a single *Hey Jude* by Paul McCartney on one side and *Revolution* by John Lennon on the other.

In 1968, Paul McCartney visited his fellow Beatle John Lennon at his house. Paul found John's five-year-old son crying. When he asked him what was wrong, Julian, who everyone called Jules, stated that "My mom and dad are getting divorced." Paul sat down at John's piano and started singing "Hey Jules don't make it bad, take a sad song and make it better, remember to let her in to your heart and you can start to make it better." When Lennon heard him singing to his young son he told him "Hey Jude sounds better that "Hey Jules". McCartney said yes, it does, adding "St. Jude is the patron saint of lost causes." My favorite line in the song however is "For well you know that it's a fool who plays it cool by making his world a little bit colder." A nice reminder to us all.

A song of acceptance and understanding and open mindedness and tolerance with a melody that sweeps us along. We miss a lot of love and life when we are closed minded, I believe open minded people see a lot more beauty in the world.

The flipside of the single was a call to action! *Revolution* by John Lennon. With a screaming guitar intro followed by Lennon screaming

"You say you want a revolution
Well you know
We'd all want to change the world"

Two songs. Two perspectives. Two world views. Two geniuses telling us their thoughts about that momentous year 1968.

Keep an open mind!

Keep opening those doors!

Keep it up!

# 14. Is "school" getting in the way of your education?

Don't let school get in the way of your education.

School is a metaphor for your daily routine—what you have to do.

Education is what you get to do.

When did you overcome "school" to further your "education"?

Are you, or were you, that student who would try anything to get out of going to school? Why was that? What were you searching for?

I was that high school student.

For years, I had made a big deal about snow days, and how quickly administrators would cancel school. I'd ramble on about when I was a kid and we had to walk through a foot of snow, uphill both ways, without shoes, at twenty degrees below zero—and we liked it. I would tell my classes that if school was ever canceled, they should check their phones because my lecture would be on their voice mail. If my line was busy, I'd tell them to keep calling back until they got through—"Remember, I have one hundred and fifty students listening." This is how they could keep up and not miss anything—just listen to my recorded lecture on the phone. I often wondered if any students had taken me seriously.

One day, school was canceled but teachers still had to come in. When I got to school, three students were waiting outside my classroom. They refused to believe that school was canceled.

"Our education should never be compromised," they passionately proclaimed. They were dead serious.

I unlocked my classroom, and we spent the entire hour discussing recent supreme court decisions. Obviously, they had remembered my constant admonition "to not let school get in the way of your education." They gave new meaning to the phrase Snow Day: "Do not let snow get in the way of your education."

A lesson that was not part of the lesson plan:

Do Not Let School Get in the Way of Your Education!

Truly!

What is your favorite memory of "skipping" school and learning more that day than you would have in a week of traditional classes?

Now, as a state senator, when I run across young people at the Minnesota capitol building—pages, tourists, demonstrators or visiting students—I always ask, "Why are you not in school?" Usually, they look down sheepishly, trying to think of the right answer. Before they can reply, I thank them, "For not letting school get in the way of your education." More often than not, this produces a knowing smile.

Go out and do the things you have always wanted to do, even if they seem undoable. Just don't stand still. Lewis Carrol wrote in *Alice's Adventures in Wonderland*, "Why, sometimes I've believed as many as six impossible things before breakfast."

Information and mindfulness are as important as imagination and mindlessness. Try for as many new experiences as you can have every day— even, perhaps, before breakfast. Routine has its place, but not at the cost of complacency. When we stop exploring, we grow old.

Bob Dylan once sang this lyric: "Those not busy being born are busy dying." My grandma attended Bob Dylan's Bar Mitzvah. When a song by Dylan came on the radio, she would tell me that "He couldn't sing then either." Those not busy being born are busy dying—indeed!

To think outside the box, you need to live *without* the box.

Nowhere on my Undertakings list is a TV show, Facebook page, Tweet or website. You may be amused, amazed, entertained, even informed by techno-traps like these, but you will never be truly astonished by anything that appears on a screen. You will never experience awe.

I'm ashamed to admit that I watched every episode of the *Sopranos*—over fifty hours of television! I could have learned to play the ukulele or how to juggle bowling balls or to speak a foreign language in that time.

Remove the screens that are blocking your vision.

Is watching TV, surfing the web or playing a game on your mobile device really what you want to do with this particular moment? This hour? This day?

What would your perfect hour look like?

If a deceased friend or relative could come back for one precious and priceless hour, what would you do with them?

What do you think they'd want to do for that hour? Play a video game? Check their Facebook status? Tweet friends? Chill?

I thought so.

When I was a young man, I knew three female roommates who had lived in my hometown of Superior, Wisconsin. They had all moved to a house just a couple miles from me in South Minneapolis. I hoped to ask one of them on a date. When they called and asked if they could borrow my TV to watch the space shuttle take off, of course I jumped at the opportunity. I don't know what is most amazing in this tale—that three women did not own a TV, that people used to watch space shuttle take-offs and landings, or that I could carry my TV on the bus to their house. Anyway, the next day I dropped off my TV and explained that I would pick it up in a few days. I believed I'd get a date out of this generous act.

A few days later, I went to pick up my TV. One of the roommates answered the door and said, "Cwod, come on in. Let me get your TV—it's in the closet."

I was perplexed. Why was my television in the closet and not the centerpiece of their living room?

"We kept it in the closet," she told me, "and brought it out when we needed it, just like the vacuum cleaner."

I was in love. This woman already knew what I was just beginning to learn—that we will never make a difference in this world from a seat in front of a television—or the screen du jour, for that matter.

I often asked my students, "How many of you have cable or satellite?" Predictably, most would raise their hands. Then I'd ask why anyone would pay money to have their life stolen from them.

Karl Marx stated that "Religion is the opiate of the masses, it dulls your senses."

I think today Marx would say, "I was wrong—religion is not the opiate of the masses, it's television that dulls our senses."

When I first heard about MTV unplugged, I got excited. I thought it was going off the air. I thought, *Now if only ESPN and TNT would go unplugged.* I recently heard that the average home spends seven hours a day watching television. At just two hours per day, that comes out to be 728 hours a year—in other words, thirty days! Think about what you could be doing with those thirty days.

Don't get me wrong, I love a good Packers vs. Vikings game or sitting with Patti on our couch watching an episode of "Our Show." But to spend over two hours every day in front of a TV is simply squandering our existence. People watching television show less brain activity than people who are sleeping. At least, when we're sleeping, we are dreaming! Watching television burns fewer calories than any other activity except death. (The more I think about it, watching television may very well be a slow death.)

I often tell people, "I will have plenty of time to watch TV when I'm old, can't walk, and I'm in an assisted living facility." By then I don't think I will have missed anything good.

I remember in class talking about "TV-Free Week." I was ranting, "Try and go a week without television!" The next day, one of my students came back and told me the following story.

"I went home yesterday," he said, "and I took all of our TVs to my grandpa's house for TV-Free Week. My mom came home and said, 'This will be fun!' Then my dad came home and said, 'Go get our TVs back!'"

I wondered how that family drama played out. When I told my twelve-year-old son about my rant in class, his reply was, "Tell them about the TV-Free Month we have to go on every summer when we're on a family road trip."

Rather than ask, "What are you binge-watching right now?" ask the next person you meet "What are you reading for pleasure right now?" Observe their facial expressions when they try to process that question. By the way, have an answer to that question in case anyone asks you!

Many people live lives of calmness waiting to find out why they were born. They spend their time in front of their screen of choice waiting for that AHA!—that transformative moment when they scream, "So that is why I was born."

I have a little secret to reveal. In the history of humankind, almost nobody has ever uttered the words, "I figured out why I was born while watching television." Yet, reading a great novel or a riveting memoir—now that can produce a genuine AHA! You will never make a difference as a spectator.

Show up and participate in life.

I once had a sign on my door that called my classroom a "CELL PHONE FREE" zone. I did not want my students looking up the answer. I wanted them thinking and pondering and reflecting. Our cell phones have become an appendage rather than a tool—a worldwide addiction! Whenever we are searching, we go to the Internet and our phones for the answer.

I was in Cuba a couple years ago. They had very limited WIFI. People still stand around in circles laughing and having conversations.

I was in a village in Mexico that still had no road into it. You could only get there by boat, and they had just recently gotten electricity. When I asked a local woman how electricity had changed her life, she replied, "Our children no longer listen to us."

Did you let school get in the way of your education?

Are you still letting school get in the way of your education?

# 15. Are you living a fully examined life?

Living a fully examined life is living a most noble life.

I introduced my students to Socrates with a painting, by the French artist David, of the "Death of Socrates." It was the first reproduction of a painting I had ever purchased and it hung in my apartment for a few years before finding its way into my classroom. Every year I go through a series of insights about, Socrates, our first western philosopher, discussing the meaning behind some of his assertions like:

An unexamined life is not worth living.
Know thyself.
Question everything.
Never have blind faith.

I would tell my classes that Socrates was once charged with "corrupting the youth," at that time punishable by death. Teaching students to think for themselves, to reach their own insights and inquiries, to analyze and synthesize—this was against the state mandate of what Socrates was supposed to teach. He was given the choice of continuing his teaching of the state-sanctioned curriculum or face execution. Courageously, he chose the latter, believing that death would be more honorable and virtuous than living a life in which he could not question everything. He became the first western philosopher to die for his convictions.

Is the search for wisdom worth your time? Socrates believed it was worth his life! He certainly practiced what he preached. An unexamined life is not worth living. A fully examined life is the most noble of lives.

This was Socrates' philosophy of teaching. It was also Cwod's philosophy of teaching.

I frequently asked students rhetorical questions, challenging their core beliefs. I would play devil's advocate to make sure all sides to every issue were considered. My students would do the same to me.

I taught American history and American government to high school students for over thirty years. I believed that students should have an intelligent, well-considered opinion after an in-depth analysis about any issue—even tough ones like gun control, the death penalty, school prayer, abortion or Pokémon. No matter what the current event or contentious topic was, I always explained, "You need to figure it out!"

Figure out which side you are on. Figure out the pros and cons. Figure out what your place is in the grand scheme of things. Figure out what the gods have in store for you. Just figure it out!

One day, after a very spirited discussion on some controversial topic, a student said to me, "You always seem to be telling us that we need to figure it out."

After a long and awkward pause, she proceeded to politely ask me if I had "figured it out" yet.

My first thought was, "Wow, how dare this young woman subtlety confront me with a little dose of my own medicine." I know she was not asking me if I had figured out a particular topic. She was asking me, a fifty-seven-year-old man, if I had "figured it out" yet in a more general sense.

A voice inside my head asked, "Cwod, do you practice what you preach?"

As an American government teacher, I got my share of student questions like "What is your favorite color?" or "What time does this class end?" or "Why is abbreviated such a long word?" or "Will this be on the test?" However, it was far more common to get questions that were more meaningful, provocative and worthy of discussion. So, when this young lady asked me, "Have you figured it out yet?" that was a meaningful and provocative question.

I honestly replied, "No, I have not figured it out." Then, after an awkward pause, I added, "As of yet!"

I looked at her, a little dissatisfied with my own answer, and asked if she had figured it out yet.

She looked at me sadly and said, "No, I haven't either."

We continued to look at each other, both disappointed with our answers. Then she asked, "Do we ever figure it out?"

"I'm not sure."

She asked if I knew anyone who had figured it out.

My mind raced with appropriate teacherly examples of candidates—Albert Einstein, Eli Wiesel, William Shakespeare, Barak Obama, Eleanor Roosevelt and numerous other philosophers, presidents, prophets and poets. After a long pause, I finally said, "I do not believe so. Perhaps none of us truly ever figures it out."

I then asked her if she thought anyone had ever figured it out?

Her reply came quickly. "Malala," she said, referring to a girl who at the age of seventeen had recently won the Noble Peace Prize. "She seems to have figured it out."

I looked at this young lady in wonder and amazement. All I could offer at this point in the conversation was this final thought: "In our quest for figuring it out, understand that most of us will never figure it out, but we must never stop striving to figure it out. After all, who knows—you may be among the few destined to figure it out."

A student once wrote to me, "Before your class, I thought I had figured it all out, Now, having been through your class, I've found that there is so much more to figure out." Truly!

Do you believe any of us ever "figure it out?"

If the answer is no, why does "it" continue to allude us?

If the answer is yes, by what methods and means can we help each other figure it out?

I had the opportunity to help young people develop into citizens who would make Franklin, Jefferson and Madison proud. What an honor that was. I believe that teachers must stimulate in their students a passion for lifetime learning and an enthusiasm for lifetime living. My enthusiasm for life spilled into my lessons and onto my students. "Enthusiasm" is a Greek word that means "to be inspired." People used to tell me I was very enthusiastic about whatever I was teaching. Well, MY students inspired ME.

I often accused students of being addicted to SOMA. For those unfamiliar with Huxley's *Brave New World*, SOMA was the daily dose of medicine administered to the masses so they would not worry or think about what was happening. I would often rant about how we have become addicted to that day's video or Tweet or Facebook post. About how our senses had been dulled by a variety of screens. About how we no longer think for ourselves and have become guilty of groupthink. I had a banner in my room which read: "Are You Addicted To SOMA?"

One morning, after the previous day's SOMA rant, I arrived at my classroom to find a poster on my door. In bold colors, a student had written: "Cwod's Classroom is Rehab for Soma Addicts." It stayed on my door for the rest of my career. I never did find out who placed it there.

What is the SOMA addiction that is preventing you from reaching:
Your purpose?
Your destiny?
Your self-actualization?

We must all help our young people build a passion, an eagerness, for their own learning. Our youth have an inherent desire to ask questions. "What's this?" and "How does this work?" are among every child's first questions. Why do so many of us stop asking questions?

I wanted my students to:
Question everything.
Have an opinion and a voice on every issue.
Become wiser with every day.
Try to figure out why they were born and how will they leave the world a better place.
Discuss ideas and events rather than possessions and people.

I taught with a quest-for-knowledge approach, encouraging my students and myself to question everything. This always leads to a more informed and involved citizenry.

When my son was eight years old, I asked him what his favorite toy was. He responded, "My mind."

Often, on the first day of class, some of my students would plop down in their seats and look at me with an expression that commanded, "Entertain me." Instead, I wanted them to arrive with expressions that said, "My mind is here and anxiously awaiting intellectual stimulation, so get my synapses firing and exploding, please!"

How do you get your synapses firing?

What do you find intellectually stimulating?

The assignments I had students do were designed to make me think or make me smile. This reminds me of a student who came up to me before class and asked, "Do you think I should be punished for something I did not do?"

"Of course not," I said.

He replied, "Good. I didn't do today's homework."

I did not fall for that one again.

On the first day of another class, I was explaining the class rules and ended with, "If you have to go to the bathroom, raise your hand."

A student in the back row asked, "How will that help?"

So, I ask, are you living a fully examined life? Have you figured it out?

# 16. Do you focus on people's strengths?

**W**hy do we focus on each other's weaknesses and imperfections rather than each other's strengths and perfections?

My grandmother always told me: "You can catch more flies with honey than you can with vinegar." Perplexed, I wondered, "Who wants to attract flies?" Years later, I realized what she was getting at.

Parents and colleagues often asked me why I never complained about my students. Frankly, I was tired of hearing others demean our young people by saying, "Today's kids are horrible," or "Today's kids are so disrespectful," or "Today's kids do not _____ as well as they used to!"

My usual response to these disparaging comments was, "Today's students are less racist, less sexist and less homophobic than they were when I started teaching."

There are so many wonderful things to say about today's young people. Besides, why not focus on their strengths and what they do well rather than what they suck at.

A well-known teacher once said: "Children today love luxury. They have bad manners, contempt for authority, show disrespect to their elders ... they no longer rise when elders enter the room. They contradict their parents, chatter before company, gobble up dainties at the table, cross their legs and are tyrants over their teachers."

That teacher was Socrates 2400 years ago!

Another teacher once said: "A society that points out people's weaknesses is a society in decline."

That teacher was me 2400 years later.

We are tearing down the statues and memorials of the past. We are exposing the heroes of the past for their warts and wounds rather than for their patriotic sacrifice and service. Maybe the reason we are disgracing these historical heroes is due to our own lack of greatness. I wonder what Freud would say?

It seems as though:

It is much easier to put people's flames out instead of helping their flames burn brighter.

It is much easier to kick people when they are down than to help them get up.

It is much easier to focus on our worst moments rather than our best ones.

Oscar Wilde said: "Every sinner has a future and every saint has a past." Why are we so quick to judge and dismiss those who have made mistakes? As a teacher, I have always believed in giving people second chances. It was, I hoped, what I tried to convey to those who came through my classroom doors.

Why do we focus on each other's failings, shortcomings, and imperfections?

Why do we prefer to discuss the misfortunes and the agonies of others?

Why do we believe our candles will burn brighter if we put other people's candles out?

Why do we focus on people's weaknesses rather than their strengths?

How many of us judge the people we meet by one incident, one lone flaw, one single event, a momentary lapse of judgment? Instead, why not judge the whole person, the entire record of the individual. What if I was judged solely on that car accident forty years ago, or a few other events in my misspent youth. I wish more of us were a little more forgiving and understanding of people's failings, looking past mistakes to focus on accomplishments and successes.

One year, I had a class of seniors that was filled with students I'd had two years earlier as sophomores. Two of these students had been in a horrible car accident in which another of my students had died. They told our class about how they had been bombarded with questions about the accident—how, for their entire junior and senior years, they were known as the two kids that survived "That Accident." Teachers would know them not for their skills, talents, and ethics, but for the accident in which someone had died. They were forever linked to that one event. They knew, however, that they were much more than that accident and told me how much they were looking forward to college because then they could be judged by who they are and not by one unfortunate event. Indeed!

My love for teaching American history and American government has always been undying, unfailing, unwavering and unflinching, even when exposing all the warts, scars and open wounds. We need to teach the darkest moments as well as the shining ones.

There are statues of Christopher Columbus and Charles Lindbergh on the grounds of the Minnesota Capitol. I lead tour groups to these two statues, describing the mistreatment of indigenous peoples by Columbus and the misstatements by Lindbergh about Jews. "Should we remove these statues?" I like to ask. Usually, a few people will nod or say "yes." Then I tell them that even though Columbus and Lindbergh did and said some pretty terrible things, they changed the world. They were heroes because they did something few others were willing to do. "A society that points out people's weaknesses is a society in decline."

One year, on the last day of school, I sat at my desk doing my final grading. A senior, in jeopardy of not graduating, stuck his head into my classroom. He had never missed a day of class but also had never turned in any of his assignments. He asked me, "Did I pass?"

He knew that he didn't have enough points but was hoping that his final exam had pushed him above the failing threshold. The look on his face, though, told me he already knew the answer.

"No," I told him, "and you're one credit short overall so you won't be allowed to get a diploma or walk at commencement."

He gave me a kind of "que sera sera" expression.

"I'm sorry my class had been a waste of time for you," I said.

The young man replied, "Thank you, that's what I expected. But for the record, it was far from a waste of time and I'll never forget you or this class."

At that moment I looked at him and thought, *You just spent nine weeks in my class, did not do anything, did not receive credit, will not walk at graduation, will now have to go to summer school—and you believe that this class you just failed was worthwhile? Wow*!

He may have passed my class after all.

Let's judge others on their successes rather than their failures.

Let's judge others when they are at their strongest rather than their weakest.

Let's judge others on their strengths instead of their weaknesses.

Imagine a news channel that focused on people's strengths rather than their weaknesses. That would really be something!

Maybe it's time to reverse course and point out the best in each of us rather than the worst. Will you give it a try?

# 17. Do you put enough time, energy, and effort into your friendships?

No one is "lucky" to have friends. It requires a great deal of time, energy and effort. When it comes to friends, we really do reap what we sow.

One day, a girl friend (but not a girlfriend) called me at six-thirty in the evening and asked if I was interested in going to a concert with her. I was cleaning offices at that time in my life and was exhausted after a ten-hour day, so I told her, "I'm really just too tired."

"My boyfriend stood me up," she confessed, "and I'll give you his ticket for free." At that point in my life, this offer very tempting, so I thought for a second and then replied, "I'm so sorry but I,m really exhausted right now."

Then she begged. "Pleeeeease. I bought this ticket and I want you to have it."

I said, "Thanks, but not tonight. Just too tired out."

She continued to coax me into accepting the ticket.

"It's already six-forty," I told her. "?How would I ever get to the concert by eight? I haven't got a car."

"The bus!" she said, then proceeded to tell me when the bus would pass my apartment, when to transfer onto the bus she'd be riding, and when we should arrive at the venue.

"Wow!" I said. "You figured out all those bus times and transfers for me?" Before she could answer I told her, "Trouble is I'm just too tired to go." In the pause that followed, I decided to satisfy my curiosity about the concert, so I asked, "Who's performing that has you so excited for me to see tonight?"

"Bob Marley," she said.

"Who?"

"Bob Marley!" she said, raising her voice.

"Is that the guy from *A Christmas Carol*?"

"NO!" she yelled. "He plays reggae music.

I had never heard of reggae, so I told her, "Well, I'm still too tired."

Before she conceded defeat, she went for the coup de grâce by promising to buy me a pizza after the concert.

"Can you give me those bus times again?" I asked.

We arrived at the venue and she had really good seats, something I was not used to as a young man. When the lights dimmed, out walked Bob Marley. Five thousand people stood up as though God himself had just appeared on stage. For the next few hours, I was transformed by this man's music. I had never seen or heard anything quite like it. The only concerts I had attended were by the likes of Deep Purple, Foghat and BTO—great concerts, but not life changing. This one, though, changed me as a person. From that point on I would no longer just scream at concerts—I would sit/stand and listen/reflect. It changed how I approached music because now I was seeking meaning from it. My friend, who just happened to be a girl, had given me a new and unexpected experience that would have been missed if I had stayed home and rested in my comfort zone.

Oh, the pizza and the friendship were great too.

I should have never told a friend I was too tired!

Years later, a student handed me a note from an old friend of mine who I had not seen for many years. The student told me, "My mom works with this guy named Ned who said he went to Hebrew school with you." The note simply said, "Steve, it's Ned. Let's get together soon."

I put the note on my desk, meaning to call soon, perhaps when I wasn't so tired. But life got in the way. A few weeks later I found out he had died.

What if I had called him and we had talked? Did he want to tell me about a medical condition? Did he need some support from an old friend? I will never know. But I know that I failed as a friend. I kept that note on my desk as a daily reminder of what truly matters.

A few years ago, a dear friend of mine had a son who died. People all around him came forward in an outpouring of love and support— I'd never seen anything like it. Someone said to me "He's lucky to have so many friends."

I immediately shot back. "There is no 'luck' in having friends. You have to work really hard at it." There was no better friend; he would stop everything if you needed something. The reason he had so many friends was because he had worked at being a friend for years. He was never too tired.

How was school today? How was work today? How was your day? If your response to these questions is, "I made some new friends" or "I was busy 'making' friends" or "I spent some time with old friends," then you had a great day. It has been documented that the happiest people are those that are constantly meeting and interacting with people. There are seven billion people in thousands of locations just waiting for you to show up.

Meet someone new every day. Make it a priority. Friends are worth looking for.

We are, after all, your species!

Human bonds are the true source of happiness. We do not need more money, we need more friends. We do not need more screen time—we need more kindred spirit time.

It's a fact that women live longer than men. Visit a nursing home and notice the male-to-female ratio. Why women live longer than men has never been a mystery to me. They have strong and solid friendships.

During my lecture on Thoreau and Emerson, I would usually show the painting *Kindred Spirits* by Asher Durand. It shows two individuals standing on an overlook in the wilderness discussing, most likely, the meaning of life—or perhaps, more importantly, how does one have meaning in their life. After considering the painting, I would ask my students, "Who is your soul mate? Who is your kindred spirit?"

Lately I have been doing a lot of reflecting on all my friends and family members who have died. (My mother-in-law just passed away.) It is almost always a person's laugh that I miss the most. So many of my dear friends had infectious laughs and how I miss hearing their laugh after they are gone. Thirty years after a friend died, I can remember his laugh more than his voice.

A good friend had just lost his twenty-year-old son after a lengthy battle with depression. At the funeral, everyone gathered in the reception area while my friend, alone in the chapel, stood by his son's casket looking defeated and depressed. I walked up to him and told an off-color joke—a risk, but one I was willing to take. He might have punched me and called me an insensitive SOB, or he could have wiped the tears from his eyes and smiled. I awaited his response.

He smiled and said, "Thanks, I really needed that."

Do not just make yourself happy—make others happy. Even if you have to leave in order to do it.

I once got a flat tire when I hit a fork in the road. I brought the tire into the shop and was charged twenty dollars to fill it with free air. When I asked about the charge, the attendant shrugged and said "You know, inflation."

After that, I needed a pick-me-up, so I went to a coffee shop and parked in a space with a small sign that read, "FINE FOR PARKING." When I came out, a policeman was writing a ticket. Evidently, we disagreed on the meaning of FINE.

He inspected my license and said, "You wear corrective lenses, it says here."

I told the officer, "I have contacts."

"I don't care who you know," he said, "I'm still giving you a ticket." But I digress.

When I was a young dad, friends asked if I could babysit their four-year-old son for a few hours. I said yes. He was the same age as my son. After the parents left, their son disappeared. I frantically ran outside thinking he may be running down the street after his mother's car but he was not there. As I turned to face the house, I breathed a sigh of relief. The little boy's head was sticking out of a window well where he was hiding.

I walked up to him and asked, "Why are you hiding?"

He said, "I don't want to hear any more of your jokes, Cwod."

Now you know how my students must have felt.

The very last words the Beatles would ever put on vinyl were in the song "The End." The lyrics were: "And in the end, the love you take is equal to the love you make."

The legacy of The Beatles is this:

They sang about love. The songs make you feel good and they make your heart stronger. Songs about alienation and angst are called for at times. Songs about depression and despair are sometimes needed. So are songs about anger and annoyance. But songs about living and loving are *always* necessary.

That's why we have:

*Love Me Do, All My Loving, All You Need is Love, Can't Buy Me Love, She Loves You,* and many more.

If you put time, energy and effort into your friendships, there is always a big payoff. After all, some things in life you can only get... With a Little Help from My Friends.

# 18. Do you treat everyone as if it were their last day?

What if we went about every day of our life as if it were our last? What if we treated everybody we met as if it was their last day on earth?

All of the words, in all of the Harry Potter books, add up to just over 1,000,000 words. 6,000,000 Jews were murdered in the Holocaust. My mom and I lived with her parents until I was twelve. They raised me in a Jewish household, where the memories of the Holocaust were never far from my grandparent's thoughts. Both had fled the horrors of anti-Semitism in Europe.

My grandma taught me to always be kind to others.

My grandpa taught me to learn from the past, so we do not repeat our mistakes.

I learned to take time to listen to our elders and learn from them.

The Holocaust is a wonderful teaching opportunity. I not only taught the Holocaust to my students, I have also taught community education classes about the Holocaust.

As a twenty-one-year-old, I vagabonded through Europe at the height of the Cold War. I had wanted to visit Auschwitz. I take that back, I needed to visit the world's largest cemetery at Auschwitz, but the authorities would not allow a young American into Poland, which was on the other side of the Iron Curtain. I did get to Dachau, because it was on the west side of the wall. Auschwitz would have to wait.

Years later, I was accepted into a program that included a month-long tour of Poland and Israel, also studying the Holocaust with survivors, rescuers, a few "employees" of the camps, and researchers. We visited death camps, ghettos, shtetels, museums and monuments. When I returned, people asked me how my vacation was. I explained that it was not a vacation, but rather a journey to discover the human spirit. I had thought that finally getting to Auschwitz twenty-five years later would be a final capstone on a part of my life. Instead, it just added a cornerstone to another chapter.

I have now taken students to Auschwitz twice. Both times, as we depart on our bus, I let each student tell the group how they were feeling. Their comments are memorable and meaningful. Some students were literally speechless. "Absolutely no words to describe my feelings," pretty much summarizes the general feeling. One young woman in tears simply said, "I wish my mom was here."

During my first visit to Warsaw, I found two memorials to Janusz Korczak, and later discovered another one in Jerusalem. I had never heard of him. All the memorials to him depict a man huddled around a bunch of children. He was the Dr. Seuss of his time—a children's doctor and writer. He opened an orphanage for Jewish children in the ghetto after the Nazis took over Poland. When the Nazis liquidated the ghetto, they sent all the children to Treblinka to be murdered in the gas chambers. The Nazis told Korczak that because of his status within the community he was free to go. But he could not abandon his children. So he stayed. He, along with two hundred orphan children, were murdered at the Treblinka death camp. He could have saved himself, but he chose to provide comfort to the children right to the very end. A profile in courage, indeed!

After presenting the story of Janusz Korsczak in class, I would often look out at my students and ask them to put themselves in my shoes for a minute. Then I would say, "If 'The Man' came to the door right now and said they were gathering up all my students for "resettlement" and I fully knew they were being rounded up to be murdered... And if 'The Man' said to me, 'Mr. Cwodzinski, you're a well-known figure in the community so you don't have to accompany your students...' Well, would I say, ;Whew, that was close!' Or would I accompany you students to the death camp?" I extended my arms outward toward my class. "Would I save myself, or would I go with you to provide aid and comfort?" I still wonder.

Treat everybody you meet as though it was their last day on earth.

God, I loved teaching!

I once met a Holocaust survivor who told me the following story about being a Jew in Nazi Germany: "One day, the principal came on the school intercom and said that we Jews were undeserving of an education, and that we were to be sent home immediately, never to come back. Any child who tried to educate themselves, and any teacher that tried to teach them, would be met with swift and certain punishment." The survivor told me how they had to form secret schools and find teachers willing to teach them with stolen textbooks.

After I told my students this story, I asked "If the principal came on the intercom right now and said, 'The [*insert group here*] need to leave school immediately because they are unfit to learn, and they must never come back.' Would those students leave school shouting "PARTY TIME!" and high-fiving each other? Or would they be trying to figure out how to secretly further their education. If your group was named, would you be yelling "yippee" and "huzzah?" Who among you would start plotting and planning how to continue your education?

I asked my students to speculate which teachers on the staff would risk their careers, even their lives, to secretly teach them.

I emphatically state that I'd proudly add my name to that list!

I once had a student who went to Auschwitz with me and the next year accompanied me to Israel. After we left the Holocaust Memorial in Jerusalem, he said to me, "Last summer at Auschwitz, I saw the horror of humanity, and I was ashamed. Today, I saw the honor of humanity and I'm so very proud. You led me to see the worst, and then to see the best in our species."

It causes such pain to see the blue stains on the gas chamber walls at Majdanek. To look back at the entrance to Auschwitz from the end of the train tracks. To imagine Anne Frank's voice while staring out the window of her hidden annex. To gaze at the ashes and bone in the ovens at Dachau.

I would ask, Would you, like the Holocaust survivors, have the will to live, the will to carry on, the will to see it through one more day even though you had already lost everything?"

I always began my Holocaust lecture this way: "No one ever died at Auschwitz and Dachau." This would provoke some quizzical looks—until I pronounced: "They were murdered!"

I like to tell the stories of survivors I've met. Some were victims, some heroes. Their stories leave me searching for meaning to my own existence. One elderly woman found out she was pregnant shortly after the war ended. She asked her doctor for an abortion because she couldn't handle the cry of a baby after she had heard so many babies crying as they and their mothers were herded into the gas chambers. The doctor told her he would not perform an abortion, so on her own she tried many different methods to abort her fetus. Some were rather gruesome. As she told us, "nothing worked," she held up a photo of a young man in an Israeli military uniform. "This is my boy, who I tried to abort. I am so very proud of him."

There are 21,000 trees planted in Israel along a walking path called the Avenue of the Righteous. A tree has been planted for every individual who was proven to be among the "Righteous Among the Nations." These are individuals who exhibited the following virtues:

Decent, Upright, Upstanding, Honorable, Virtuous, Righteous

None of these 21,000 courageous individuals who have been honored with a tree ever said: "How will this decision adversely affect me?"

The most famous tree is probably Oscar Schindler's. One of the last scenes in the movie *Schindler's List* shows him being presented a ring engraved with these words from the Talmud: "He who saves one life saves the world entire."

At this moment, can you say, "I have climbed to the summit of humanity?" Have you left us all here on earth better and brighter than you found us? There is a relevant Hebrew expression, "Tikkun olam," that can be loosely interpreted as: "Be kind to others and repair this world." Is what you have done the best you can do? Be a profile in courage!

What is the most courageous thing you have ever done?
What is the most courageous thing you failed to do?
When you ask what one person can do, remember Oscar Schindler.

Standing in front of Schindler's tree along the Avenue of the Righteous, I experienced a major epiphany. Why not have an Avenue of the Righteous at our high school? This could be a walking path where we plant a tree every year in honor of a senior who did the most to benefit humanity. My idea fell on deaf ears, of course, but maybe someday a high school in Minnesota will adopt my proposal. What a wonderful message this would send our youth.

"Mitzvah" is a Yiddish word that means "a meritorious act." There is an old Jewish proverb that states: "The reward of a mitzvah? Another Mitzvah!" Good deeds know no boundaries. They never end. So, do some good for someone today.

I often tell the story of fifteen-year-old Petr Ginz who was murdered in the Terezin concentration camp. Before he was gassed, his personal mission in the camp was to keep hope alive—and fear away—in all the children. He started a newspaper to give purpose and hope to those destined to die. Of the fifteen thousand imprisoned children, less than one hundred survived. After my Holocaust lecture one term, a student handed me a note that read: "I am proud to belong to the same species as Petr. Thanks for changing who I am."

A memorial exists in Duluth, Minnesota, to three teenage men who were hung from a lamp post for a crime they did not do by a crowd of five thousand. It is a somber memorial. On it is this quote by Albert Einstein engraved in stone: "The world is a dangerous place, not because of those that do evil, but those that look on and do nothing."

Near the end of my Holocaust lesson, I briefly tell the story of Robert Kennedy's remarks on the day Martin Luther King was murdered. In his speech, he recited this poem by Aeschylus:

Even in our sleep, pain which cannot forget
falls drop by drop upon the heart,
until, in our own despair,
against our will,
comes wisdom
through the awful grace of God.

That is why I teach and study the Holocaust.

As the bell rang ending each Holocaust lesson, I always displayed the following words on the screen:

I tell this story not to weaken you but to strengthen you!

This may have been the only lesson I delivered where my students were simultaneously kicked in the stomach and kicked in the ass.

After I retired from teaching, I embarked on a campaign to be elected state senator. During this campaign, I encountered a man on the street who asked me how the campaign was going. I said it was going well, and then he said, "You had our son in school. He really enjoyed your class. However, we are Republicans. and you're a Democrat."

I told him thanks and gave my "I do not want to live in a one party state speech," and we parted. A few houses down the street, a woman ran up to me. It turned out it she was the man's wife. She also thanked me for teaching her son, then played a message on her phone that she had kept from a few years back. The message was her son telling her, "I love you, Mom." She told me he called and left her those wonderful words on her voice mail—unfortunately, all too rare for teenage boys—after hearing my Holocaust lecture. She had kept that message all these years. As we both started getting a little *verklempt*, she leaned into me and whispered, "My husband and I will both be voting for you."

That made my day as much as her son's phone call had continually made hers.

Treat everybody you meet as though it was their last day on earth!

# 19. How many heart attacks have you given today?

Bring on a heart attack—the kind where the recipient grabs their chest with pride rather than pain.

On the last day of school, long after the building had cleared out of students, I walked out of my room to find one of my seniors cleaning out her locker with cleaning supplies. I told her that custodians spend all summer cleaning out the lockers, so she should stop and go have fun with her classmates. But she didn't want the custodians to have to clean out her locker. "Besides, I am done now," she said.

I just smiled at her.

As she finished cleaning up, she placed a sealed envelope into the locker, which would be assigned to an incoming freshman in the fall.

"What's in the envelope?" I asked.

She said, "The real reason I didn't want anybody else to clean out my locker is so I could leave this note for the next student who'd use it. The note has all my advice and wisdom on how to have a successful four years here."

I grabbed my chest—not in pain, but with pride. She had just given me a heart attack, one of those drop-a-jaw moments when you are joyfully astonished! These so-called "heart attacks" happened to me more and more often after that day, probably because I started looking for them.

One time in class, after the bell rang, a student started puking into the trash can. The other students all rushed out of the room. This was the first day of class, and I'm sure the entire episode was embarrassing for the student.

Just then, a girl started comforting the student by rubbing his back. I called the nurse and the janitor, and then stood outside the door to prevent the next class from entering. As the chaos wound down, the nurse led the sick student away, and the girl started gathering her things.

I asked her, "How long have you two been dating?"

She laughed and said, "I've never seen him before today."

God, I loved teaching!

I remember when we had a drunk driving simulation at our high school. Up to that point, I had not yet told my students about my accident—I guess it was still too fresh on my mind. We were all herded out to the stadium to sit and observe a drunk driving re-enactment.

When we got back to the classroom, I sat at my desk emotionally exhausted and intellectually spent. For the only time in my teaching career, I told my class to take lunch early. The students looked around, assuming I was kidding, or maybe thinking it was a trick. One student after another slowly left for lunch—hoping, I'm sure, that I wouldn't change my mind. For the first time ever, I could not do my job.

I was sitting in the classroom alone with my thoughts when the door slowly opened. A ninth-grade girl tentatively entered, sadly looked at me and then asked, "Are you OK, Mr. Cwodzinski?"

How in the world do you raise a child to be so caring and perceptive about another human? I am in awe of people like that girl. Or maybe this was an example of transcendentalism—access to a body of knowledge that transcends the senses. This ninth-grader had an IQ beyond her years, not an Intelligence Quotient but rather and Internal Quality—one's youthfulness, energy, devotion, happiness, kindness, optimism and enthusiasm. You know, that undefinable thing we can't measure, nor do I believe we should want to.

How do we raise kids like these?

There is a theory called tabula rasa that suggests individuals are born without built-in mental content, and therefore all knowledge comes from experience or perception. Are we truly a blank slate, then? If so, how and when did my son learn that picking up a gentleman's cane was not only the right thing to do, but the responsible, selfless and gallant thing to do?

When my son was about three years old, his feet did not touch the floor of the café where we were eating. Suddenly, an elderly gentleman across the aisle dropped his cane and couldn't reach it. My son put down his fork, climbed out of his seat, picked up the man's cane and handed it to him before returning to his chair to resume eating. He did all this without saying a word. As you can imagine, I was stunned. How did he know to do that? How did he know he needed to pick up that cane for that elderly gentleman that very moment?

We never covered that topic in Parenting 101.

Transcendentalism—a body of knowledge that truly transcends the senses. Indeed! Maybe that body of knowledge comprises all the things we do not teach in school.

Treat everybody you meet as though it was their last day on earth. Bring on a heart attack.

Never give up on our species. We all need a second chance.

Never give up on our species. We all make mistakes so forgive and make amends.

Never give up on our species. Together we can help people move forward, outward, upward.

In one class, I had a student who really seemed to hate me and didn't like coming to class. Suddenly, she dropped out. I was not too disappointed because she seemed so unhappy and bitter. Several years later, I was speaking at an alternative high school graduation ceremony and spotted that girl in the front row. After the ceremony, she approached me. I was half-expecting her to spit at me or to tell me to get f*cked, but she gave me a big hug, thanked me for never giving up on her, and then apologized for her classroom behavior. The power of forgiveness!

We all make mistakes, but do we learn from them?

I spent the latter half of a term looking at an empty desk that had been occupied for the first few weeks. Earlier in the term, it had belonged to a student who had taken his own life. He had sat there quietly for the first few weeks, and then suddenly he was gone. I spent the rest of that year reflecting upon that empty desk and the young man who had sat there. What did he need from me that I didn't give him? What did he need from *us*?

Maybe if I had just said, "How are you today?" or "Nice answer on the test," or maybe just smiled as he walked out the door—then would that desk still be occupied? As I thought about it, my heart sank.

Even worse than me having to stare at that empty desk was the student's parents having to look at that empty chair across their dining room table every night.

As the saying goes: "It takes a village." This one we missed.

Sometimes we reach out to people when we do not even intend to. One day I had been lecturing on MLK, and with seconds left, I shouted out a quote by King: "No person's life is worth living unless he has something worth dying for." Students frantically wrote down that quotation as the bell rang. As the last students left and I was heading for lunch and a potty stop, I noticed that one student was still sitting at her desk softly sobbing. I'm not the most sensitive person in the world—ask my wife or daughter—but a crying student always gets my sympathy.

There were no students entering the room, so I asked her what was going on?

Through her tears, she replied that she had just gotten hit with a ton of bricks and had the epiphany of a lifetime. There was a box hanging from the ceiling that I could point to whenever I found that a student was "stuck inside the box." The girl smiled briefly, then pointed at the box and said "I was stuck inside that box." When I saw her smile I knew she would be all right.

The girl told me that every night she went home from school and thought about different ways of killing herself. And every morning, she dragged herself to school for another day of misery, sadness and sorrow until she went home again to repeat the whole process. "The only thing that changes," she said, "are the different ways of killing myself."

I remember realizing that I had no training for this type of conversation, but I had to do something so I sat and listened to her. Suddenly, I worried that she was not going to be all right.

Then she told me she just had the biggest epiphany of her life. Not just a minor "Epi" but a full-blown EPIPHANY! "You know, Mr. Cwodzinski," she said, "the reason I've been thinking about suicide is because I thought I had no reason to live anymore. But as you were telling us, 'No person's life is worth living unless they have something worth dying for,' it dawned on me that my problem is not that I have nothing worth living for. It's that I have nothing worth dying for."

She repeated the words "I have nothing worth dying for," and then said, "I want to thank you for making me realize that. Now I want to live, and I'm going to continue to live, searching for something worth dying for."

I looked in her eyes and said, "Great, can I go eat now?"

She laughed, and then I walked her to the counselor's office. I thanked that young women for an amazing conversation as I said goodbye. I hope someday she invents something that improves our lives, or becomes a world leader, or becomes a great mother, or becomes a dear friend or perhaps a kind and caring teacher. As I walked down the hall, I thought, *She's going to be awesome!*

As the saying goes: "It takes a village." This one we saved.

Treat everybody you meet as though it was their last day on earth. Truly!

One time I was hauling in a box of graded papers. As I approached the door, I knew I was going to struggle with opening it. A bunch of Goth students were lounging and lollygagging at the entrance, blocking the door. *What a hassle*, I thought. Not only are my arms getting sore and I'm going to struggle with the door, but now I'll have to navigate this group of Goth knuckleheads.

Just then, two Goths opened the door for me and offered to carry my box. The next day I told all my classes about how I had pre-judged and mis-judged those kids. I looked at my students that day and said, "Thank you all for making me a better person."

I loved how teaching kids made me a better and more open-minded person. That's true as well, I think, for everyone that works with young people.

God, I loved teaching!

I had on display in my room many of the T-shirts students had made for our class trips—over twenty of them. On the last day of my career, one of my students asked what I was going to do with all the T-shirts? "Take them home, I suppose," I said.

She asked me if I would like them made into a quilt.

Before I could answer, she had gathered them up in her arms. A month later, she brought the quilt to my campaign office—a priceless act of gratitude.

How do we raise kids like these? Indeed!

I remember one time that a student brought back a suitcase filled with smashed pop cans collected during our Washington, DC, trip. The hotel did not have a recycling program, so she had filled her suitcase with smashed pop cans, rather than disposing of them in the trash.

Bring on a heart attack! Not the kind where the recipient grabs their chest with pain, but the kind where recipients grab their chests with pride and say, "I am glad I know you."

When I ran this heart attack idea by my cardiologist, he told me that it "sounds good for business." But I digress.

# 20. What do people see when they see you?

There are 400,000 words in the English Language. The average fourteen-year-old in 1950 had a vocabulary of 25,000 words. In 2000, the average vocabulary had declined to 10,000 words. When I revealed this horrible bit of information to my students, one of them belted out, "That's because we've become more efficient with our language."

I replied, "Well, you do have to be smart to be a smart ass." Then I added: "You're right, though. 'Like,' 'Uhm,' 'Whatever,' and the F-bomb have replaced 15,000 words.

Of those 400,000 words, my favorite eight are: "Thank you, I am glad I know you."

One day, I was very crabby about something, just ranting and raving, when one of my students said, "Does someone need a hug?"

I've had twelve thousand students over the years. I wish I could give every one of them a hug, a handshake, a fist bump or a pinky promise. I've learned so much from all of them. Especially from those who had a joyful and enthusiastic attitude when dealing with adversity. They always seemed to remind me of what is truly important in life.

What do people see when they see you?

What do people hear when they hear you?

How do you make others feel?

Do you bring the best version of yourself to every human interaction?

I once subbed for a colleague who told me a student was going to show a PowerPoint for the first half-hour and then told me to administer a quiz that that would take up the other second half. Easy!

So, the class began and a seventeen-year-old girl started her PowerPoint, which illustrated a brain tumor that had been discovered in her head. As she described the images on the screen, she enthusiastically said that sometimes the surgery for this kind of tumor was fatal, sometimes the patient never walks again, and sometimes they are never able to speak again. As she went from one worst case scenario to the next, her smile beamed brightly as though she was describing her spring break vacation. She finished her presentation with a huge smile and the words, "However, one thing is certain. I will be bald at prom because of my chemotherapy and radiation treatments."

I sat in awe. This young women looked upon her surgery as if it was going to be "an exciting new adventure." As she finished, I gave directions to the quiz and then led the young presenter into the hall to tell her how remarkable she was, and how her attitude and resiliency would take her far in life.

I walked back to the room and proctored the quiz, reminding the students to "Answer in complete sentences and use the five-paragraph format." Shortly thereafter, a student raised her hand and said, "I think our teacher said we only have to answer in bullet points." I looked down at the directions and realized she was right.

After I corrected my directions for the quiz, a student who had been frantically writing paragraphs the entire time looked up at me with revulsion and made that teenager sound of disgust for making her do unnecessary work. I looked at her, pointed to the screen where we had just watched the PowerPoint, and then pointed toward the door through which the cancer patient had departed.

"Did you not learn anything today?" I asked.

The student looked at me apologetically and replied, "You're right, it's not that big a deal."

God, I Loved Teaching!

I was on a plane going to DC one year, sitting next to one of my students and making small talk. She told me that when she was in fourth grade, she was diagnosed with cancer and given six months to live.

"That must have been horrible," I said.

She looked at me tearfully. "It was the best thing that ever happened to me," she said and then told me how her dad traveled a lot, and she didn't know him very well. When she received her diagnosis, he finally took time off from his job to be with her. It turned out that while she had cheated death, her father had not. He died a short time later.

She told me, "If I had not been given that diagnosis of six months to live, I may never have really known my father, and for that I am grateful." She longingly gazed out the window as she finished her thoughts.

One day in class, I was talking about JFK's Inaugural Address and the often-cited quote: "Ask not what your country can do for you, ask what you can do for your country." This is, in my opinion, perhaps the greatest definition ever of our roles in a democracy.

I told my students about how my grandparents had given me a milk glass with those words written on it. I got a little misty-eyed when I told them the story of my immigrant grandparents trying to instill in a little five-year old boy the importance of those words. I described how those two immigrants fleeing tyranny, fascism, Nazism, communism, anti-Semitism and all the other isms presented their grandson his milk every night at supper with those powerful words written on the glass. It was a stark reminder of the past for my grandparents, and a hopeful reminder of the future for their grandson.

One year, I had a student who was born "a little person." She was a bright ray of sunshine who entered my classroom and my life every day. At birth, she'd been given a tough hand to play, but she was not going to let that bring her down. Now and then, she would bring me a twelve-pack of Throwback Mountain Dew—much better than an apple. She could barely carry it, but she knew how much it meant to me. All these years later I can still hear that laugh of hers. She loved life!

After hearing my lecture about the JFK quote and my milk glass, she enthusiastically asked, "Do you still have that milk glass?"

"No, I don't," I sadly admitted. "It disappeared into the ash heap of history."

In her tone of delight and happiness, which was her mantra, she said, "You should buy another one." I replied, "What are the odds of me finding the glass?"

"Try e-Bay," another student said.

I told them I'd never bought anything on e-Bay.

Laughing, she said, "We'll help you. It will be a new experience." Even after so many years have passed, I can still see her saying this as if it had happened an hour ago.

After school, she and a friend used my computer to open up e-Bay, and within a minute they helped me find an image of the glass I had not seen in over fifty years.

I cried, literally. This became the first and last purchase I ever made on e-Bay. This is what that young woman barely four feet tall brought to my life. She was a giant among my students.

Who is a giant among all the individuals you know? Who stands the tallest?

Your attitude is your greatest asset.

Truly!

For those of you who are *Citizen Kane* fans, she helped me find my "Rosebud." I wonder what Freud would say?

What is your ROSEBUD? (Watch *Citizen Kane* if you have no idea what this means, and for God's sake, DO NOT Google it!)

Is your Rosebud in your possession, or have you lost it to the ash heap of history?

I once taught a class called Global Problems. We changed the title of the course a few years later to Global Insights, thinking it would not be such a buzz-kill. It was the late 80s then, and we learned about the AIDS epidemic, nuclear proliferation, global warming, apartheid, other cataclysmic and catastrophic subjects, as well as "Armageddon out of here." Get it?

When I used to lecture on the nuclear triad, we would discuss ICBM's, and invariably a student would ask, "What is an ICBM?"

I explained that it's either an Inter-Continental Ballistic Missile or something someone has at the North Pole—an Icy BM!

I have fond memories of a senior who loved life and loved to learn. He epitomized the joy of a great attitude, and you know how contagious that can be. He was in my first-hour class—the school day began at 7:20 a.m. He was the kind of student who would come up before class and ask, "So, what are we learning about today?" He'd also come up after class with a huge smile saying something like, "Thank you Cwod, I really didn't understand anything about the Iran-Contra affair until today." He came to class not just ready to learn but wanting to learn, and I was grateful.

Students like that are a teacher's dream come true. I was fortunate to have had so many.

Well, one day I received a memo about a meeting after school regarding a student's eye problem. I assumed it was about eyeglasses and his not liking the idea of wearing them, which would mean I'd have to tell him to "Just put on your glasses. No one will call you four-eyes, and girls will still think your cute—plus, you'll be able to see the black board."

I arrived a few minutes late to the meeting. Surprisingly, the conference was filled with a dozen adults and the grateful young man from my first hour. I sat down in a chair across from him. A man introduced himself as the family doctor and then introduced me to the rest of the adults—his parents and their doctor, his counselor and a social worker on one side of the table and on the other side his five teachers and me.

I may not be the brightest bulb on the Hanukkah Bush, but I realized this probably was not about wearing glasses.

After the introductions, the doctor explained that this young man had a rare vision condition called something unpronounceable with many syllables. When the student woke up every day, he experienced progressively less peripheral vision. Some days he detected a difference, and sometimes days or months would go by without any noticeable change. "But someday," the doctor said, "he will awaken and never see anything ever again. This could happen in a month or in a few years."

My mind was numb. I had been sitting across from this high school senior who always wore a warm smile and an expression that now seemed to say, "So, Mr. Cwodzinski, how would you play this hand I was dealt?"

The doctor asked each teacher for advice on how to proceed educationally. Should he learn to use Braille and a service dog while he can still see, or should they wait until after he is totally blind? Each teacher gave their opinion, ending with me.

"Mr. Cwodzinski, what do you think?" the doctor asked.

I laughed, not a happy laugh, but that awkward kind of laugh you emit when no other response makes any sense. This was all I had. I'm sure they all thought, *Who invited this buffoon?*

Most kids at this student's age were thinking about dances, parties, and ball games and fast cars. This kid is thinking about whether he will be able to see tomorrow. I was speechless.

So, what I said to the parents, to the counselor, the teachers, the social worker, the doctor and the young man was—absolutely nothing. I just laughed nervously. What could I offer this incredible young man? The parents looked at me in disbelief, the young man smiled kindly and my peers were incredulous.

Finally, the doctor thanked all the teachers, adding, "You are free to leave now. We'll take your advice and proceed forward from here."

I walked out with a dear friend who said that I had embarrassed myself in front of everyone in that room.

"Can you believe what just happened in there?" I said. "Do you have any idea what that kid is like in class? He walks in early every day with a smile on his face, ready to learn. He is actively and happily engaged all hour. He even thanks me as he leaves. Do you know what kind of a day brightener he is? Do you know how inspiring he is?"

She said, "Yes, I have him in class too, remember?"

I had a student that week who tried to commit suicide because she was not asked to prom. I told her I had a student kick in a locker because the combination did not work. I told her I had a student swear and verbally harass me because she did not like being told to be on time to class. I told her I'd had students attend class in foul moods because their parents did not give them the car or their clothes did not match. And here was this student who was going blind and still smiling at our meeting. "How do you raise a kid to be like that?"

She looked at me, understanding now why I had laughed, and said, "Why don't you go back in there and tell the parents what you just told me?"

And that's what I did. I walked back into the room and told the parents why I was so dumbstruck, so flabbergasted, so speechless. I repeated what I had just said in the hall and ended by telling them, "He may very well have the best vision of anyone I know."

The next morning, before school started, the student walked through my door. As usual, he was the first to arrive. He came right up to me and said, "Thanks for saying those nice things about me yesterday. My parents were so proud of me, they floated out of the building."

"That meeting was a real eye-opener for me," I said. OOOPS! My face turned seventeen different shades of red. I looked at him and I said I was sorry.

He just laughed and said, "That is a funny line. I'll have to start using it myself." Then he asked me something I will never forget, not for the rest of my life.

"What should I go see?"

Again, I was speechless. What do you tell someone what they should see before they will never see again? Wow! If this was my last day of sight, what would I want to see?

I looked at him and answered almost immediately, "Go to the art museum and study the masters. Braille cannot possibly distinguish a Rembrandt from a Renoir, a Warhol or a Van Gogh—an O'Keefe from a Frida. Then get in a car with a few friends and drive as far away from the city as you can. Find a field somewhere, lay down blankets and sleeping bags, and stare up at a starlit sky on a moonless night—the Milky Way in all its grandeur.

I give this same advice to all of you. and while you are staring at the sky, ask these questions:

What is the meaning of life?

Why am I here?

Who am I?

What makes you *you*?

Is their intelligent life out there?

Why do we park on driveways and drive on parkways?"

What was the best thing before sliced bread?

The student looked at me, smiled, and said, "Great ideas, thanks." As he walked to his desk, I knew I was watching a young man who may have been going blind, but who had the best vision of anyone I have ever known. After all, as the Beatles sang in *Strawberry Fields Forever*, "Living is easy with eyes closed, misunderstanding is all you see." His eyes were wide open.

Gratitude is a natural outgrowth of a great attitude. In fact, it is Great Attitudes which will result in such displays of Gr-attitude. A funny thing about gratitude and thankfulness is it grows and accumulates around us in direct proportion to our success in spreading it.

That night, when I got home, I made a list of the ten greatest things to behold. The ten things I just love to gaze at, to behold and admire. What are the ten things you look forward to seeing because they make you feel like you are part of something bigger than yourself? What ten things would you tell someone they really need to see if they were losing their eyesight?

The following is my list, in no particular order:

Sunrise over Lake Superior.

The Statue of Liberty.

A breaching whale at sea.

Rembrandt's *Night Watch*.

"Forget Me Nots" growing by a mountain stream.

The birth of your (or any) child.

The Grand Canyon.

The US Capitol.

The Milky Way.

Bald Eagles soaring in the sky.

If someone you knew was going blind, what would you insist they see?

What would be on your list of top ten must see experiences?

Who among all your friends and acquaintances do you believe has the greatest vision?

How do you make others feel when they see you?

What do we see when we see you?

Are we seeing the best vision of you?

Attitudes are contagious—is yours worth catching?

Strive to see what is truly vital to our existence!

# 21. Is your glass half full?

Optimism and enthusiasm ignite sparks and fuel fires. Negativity and cynicism simply put the sparks out and douse the flames. It has been estimated that we all have fifty thousand thoughts every day, and that we get to control our reactions to those thoughts. Someone once stated, "It is your attitude, not your aptitude, that will determine your altitude."

Some say I am too upbeat and positive and optimistic.

When I see light at the end of the tunnel, some say it is a train.

When I say stop and smell the roses, some say watch out for those thorns or that hornet.

When I say it is a beautiful day, some say rain is in the forecast.

When I say do someone some good today, some say no good deed goes unpunished.

When I say the glass is half full, some say the glass is half empty.

When people ask me how I remain so upbeat and optimistic, I tell them, "I can't help it. I'm short."

When they ask, "What has that got to do with anything?" I tell them that when I look up, I can only see that the glass is half full. Tall people look down and see the glass half empty."

Looking for the bright side will result in more positive outcomes than naysaying ever will!

Cinderella was an ex-student of mine. Several years after she graduated, I ran into her as we were standing in line at a film developing store. She was a few customers in front of me. I began to reminisce about her fondly, especially her years on the soccer team. She was absolutely the worst player ever! She blamed the coach for everything, complaining that he was a pumpkin, yet anyone who saw her play knew she was always running away from the ball.

Now she was standing in line while employees were frantically looking for her family photos. Cinderella just stood there smiling while the manager said, "We've looked everywhere and just can't find them."

I thought about all the people who would react to such news by screaming, "You've lost my priceless, irreplaceable family photos!" before leaving the store in a rage. Yet Cinderella just smiled. As she turned around, our eyes met, and she shouted, "Mr. Cwodzinski."

We hugged, and I asked her why she did not seem upset.

She shrugged her shoulders and said, "Someday my prints (prince) will come."

Or now that I think about it, was that my ex-student Sleeping Beauty? But I digress.

Where some see problems, I have always seen possibilities.

Where some people are filled with cynical hostility, I have always been filled with positivity.

Where some folks see snags, glitches, and complications, I have always seen potentials.

For years, many parents, students, and colleagues would ask me, an American Government teacher, "When are you going to run for public office?" I would smile and politely thank them for the suggestion. However, in the back of my head were these questions floating around: Do I practice what I preach? Do I walk the walk? Do I set a good example for my students? For over thirty years, I repeated, "Get out there and lead. Find your passion, your cause, your purpose— and lead your species toward a better world."

Then, in December of 2015, during my last year of teaching, a few members of the Democratic Party asked if I was interested in running for public office. I was flattered and intrigued, so I consulted with my family. By January, I was not only finishing my last year of teaching, I was also running a campaign against the senate minority leader.

No one told me that from January through the middle of June, my life would be in constant motion.

Until mid-June, my normal teacher routine would be grading papers and exams and preparing for two different eighty-six-minute classes every night. Prior commitments had me planning, coordinating and leading trips to Cuba, DC, and eastern Europe for over a hundred adults and students between April and June. I also had to renew my teaching licensure in case I had second thoughts about giving up teaching. Then there was packing up my classroom of thirty years, peeling layers of posters and props off the ceilings and walls, and filling out what seemed like mounds of paperwork for retirement and the school district. Oh, I also had to clean out my desk, files, discs and my computers; write teaching and education speeches and articles that I had promised for a variety of events; and host two teachers from Germany at our house for ten days. Had I lost my mind?

Wait, I'm not done. On top of all that, we were planning on downsizing, so we were busy packing up, throwing out and giving away all the stuff we had amassed over twenty-five years. When we put our house on the market, it sold in a day, which added urgency to everything else. We ended up moving into a rental townhome while looking for a permanent house.

Wait, I'm still not done. During all this, I was running in a very competitive state senate race, which was proving to be an amazing new experience. It involved door-knocking five days a week, attending fundraisers, writing campaign speeches, preparing for and speaking at twenty-eight precinct caucuses, meeting dozens of new people every day and hundreds every week.

The most eventful day of that spring was the local party convention on a Saturday morning. Two of us were seeking the party's endorsement. The convention was on the same weekend as my twentieth and final trip leading students to Washington, DC. Flights and hotel arrangements could not be changed for forty-four people, so it was a real conundrum.

That Friday, I took my students to the airport with a fellow chaperone, gave him my usual Friday night and Saturday itinerary, and told everybody, "I'll see you all around four o'clock tomorrow." The vote for endorsement would follow our speeches and canvassing, hopefully ending around noon. My flight was at one o'clock. There was no room for error. I had to win on the first ballot or I was screwed. A 60 percent vote was required to receive the endorsement.

Mercifully, the final vote was 60-40 percent on the dot! I thanked the convention and was whisked to the airport by my pre-arranged chauffeur and friend. I met my students at the Washington Monument right on schedule. They greeted me with a round of applause. On that fateful day, I was joined by many of my new friends, which was perhaps the best part of my campaign.

I had never worked harder in my life, yet it was never really work, I loved every minute of it. When I would explain or describe to someone how my day or my month had been, I would say, "There needs to be a word for positive stress." Yes, I was frizzled and frazzled beyond belief, but it was not work, it was not stress—it was a wonderful, eye-opening experience. Every day was different. Is there a word in the English language that describes: "I am so busy, I am so stressed out, I have never worked harder, and yet I am loving every minute of it!?" There has got to be a word for that—come on, lexicologists.

Deciding to run a political campaign against the senate minority leader was definitely not in my comfort zone! I had never door-knocked, asked for campaign money or sought out endorsements before. But whether I won or lost, I was having a multitude of new experiences.

Six months after I left the classroom, I was sworn in as one of the sixty-seven state senators in Minnesota.

I had imagined retirement would be somewhat different than this— perhaps lying on a beach with an adult beverage—yet I discovered something much more enriching. I am serving and representing the people of Senate District 48 in the Minnesota State Senate. And I'm loving every minute of this new experience. How could retirement top that?

Now, as I begin my fourth year as a state senator, I find myself reflecting on my new career and the wonderful people I've met. The halls and classrooms of the high school have been replaced with the halls and chambers of the state capitol. I loved my time in the classroom, and now I love my time in the stateroom. Being a senator is as great as being an educator, maybe even better. It is like being back in college, except this time, I want to learn everything the people around me are trying to teach. Also, I do not have to wait for the bell to go potty.

I am like a kid in a candy store, eyes wide open.

I love my new job. I have found my purpose for now.

I continue on my quest to solve as much of the puzzle as possible before I pass.

Oh, and I have been told, "You suck at retirement!" What a compliment.

I learned! I laughed! I loved! Therefore, I lived!

It is healthier to be smiling and laughing than to be frowning and yelling!

Love the Life you are Living! It is the only one you will ever get.

Did you learn a little today?

Did you laugh a little today?

Did you love a little today?

If yes, then you lived today.

May your glass always be half full.

# 22. Do you know your ABCs?

When we ask children, "Do you know your ABCs?" a bright smile comes across their faces as they begin to sing. I believe asking that question means much more than simply seeing whether the child can recite their ABCs. It is a metaphor for what they know, and how excited they are to show and share that with you. It is that perfect balance of learning and playing.

Next time—or how about right now— sing out, "ABCD... WXY and Z, now I know my ABCs next time won't you sing with me?" Did it make you smile? Think about why that song is so cool. It is about being joyful and being proud. It is about being mindful, being silly, building friendships.

It is about enthusiasticism.

Why do we sing our ABCs with such enthusiasticism? Maybe because we are really CONNECTING with others. That is why, when we play, we play with enthusiasticism.

When you are not sad, lonely and troubled, and you help someone that is, you are connecting.

When you make a new friend or get in touch with an old friend, you are connecting.

When you thank someone for their courage or friendship, you are connecting.

When you help the proverbial little old lady cross the street, you are connecting.

When you set up a website to help your classmates, you are connecting.

When you see to it that someone breathes a little easier, laughs a little bit harder, or climbs a little higher, you are connecting.

When you stick your finger into an electrical outlet, you are connecting.

Why were you happier as a child than you are at this moment, perhaps? Why is it if I walk into a third-grade room and say, "If you're happy and you know it clap your hands," everyone claps.

When I sais this to my seniors, they looked at me with concern.

Why do children laugh hundreds of times a day and adults just a handful?

I participated for many years in a weekend retreat for middle school students. Part of my message I delivered to those students was: "Get out there!" and "Grow" and "Take chances" and "Dare to fail." My motivational talk was followed by music and dancing into the night. During the dance, I stood around, looked interested and tried to talk the disc jockey into playing at least one Beatles song.

One year, a group of eighth grade girls asked me to dance. I gave some lame excuse about being too old, and they should just go have fun. About a half-hour later, they approached me again. Clearly, they could not tell that this old man was content just hanging and chilling. This time they pleaded: "Please come dance with us." I smiled again and said, "No thank you."

After another thirty minutes, the disc jockey announced: "This is the last dance." The same girls surrounded me and pleaded for me to dance. I politely told the young girls, "I really don't care to dance." That's when a brave and astute listener looked at me with a huge, beaming smile and said, "Have you ever danced at Prairie Fest?" Before I could answer, she belted out, "It will be a new experience!"

I danced that last dance with a huge grin and loved every minute of it.

I did that weekend retreat for middle school students for a number of years. I truly believe that I got more out of those weekends than the students did. The first time I participated, I was pumped up to try and do something, anything, that I had been putting off. On the drive home, I thought, *How could I make a difference?* and *How could I do some good?* and all the other things I had been advocating all weekend. I could hardly wait to get home and practice what I had been preaching. I arrived home at last with an epiphany.

I had inherited my grandfather's thirty-second degree Elks ring. It had rested in a safety deposit box for over twenty years. I had no idea what to do with that huge ring with a huge diamond. It was not my style. My wife, once had reminded me that the diamond would look great on her finger.

I told Patti that we were going tomorrow to get the ring out of the safety deposit box because the diamond would look more beautiful on her finger than it did in a bank vault.

If not from the enthusiasticism of fifty eighth-graders, I am sure that ring would still be in a box. As a result of those retreats, my wife got my grandpa's ring, I made a pecan pie, I started yoga and I danced with a few eighth graders. God, I miss those retreats.

During one retreat, an eighth-grader came up to me and said, "Thanks for helping me grow." A few years later, that same kid returned as a counselor, and this time said, "There was a time when you helped me realize how I could grow. Now, this weekend, I am asking myself, "How can I help others grow?"

Every time I returned from these weekend retreats, my friends would tell me, "That is so nice of you to volunteer your time and energy like that." I just smile and tell them I don't do it for the kids, I do it for me. Those eight graders pushed me and fueled me with an energy that lasted for days.

On one such retreat I coined the word "enthusiasticism." Surprisingly, it never caught on.

As I have said, play like you are a kid at the beach, the playground or the park.

Can you imagine if we all found meaning and merriment in every moment and in every manner?

When was the last time you played—and I mean played—squealing with joy and youthfulness?

If you cannot decide between two activities, choose the one you have never done before. In fact, jump at the chance.

When did you last feel a sense of enthusiasticism?

RFK, back in the 1960s, was asked about the nation's GNP and economic growth. His reply has motivated me, not just as a teacher and a senator, but as an American. He stated:

"The gross national product does not allow for the health of our children, the quality of their education or the joy of their play. It does not include the beauty of our poetry or the strength of our marriages, the intelligence of our public debate or the integrity of our public officials. It measures neither our wit nor our courage, neither our wisdom nor our learning, neither our compassion nor our devotion to our country. It measures everything, in short, except that which makes life worthwhile."

Maybe RFK was on to something. Perhaps he was asking us if we knew our ABCs?

How does one teach that? How does one test that?

Recently, I was speaking to a group of students in my new role as a state senator. They were respectful and intellectually curious as I answered their questions. Toward the end of the seminar, a young woman asked, "What do you think of standardized testing?"

I replied, "I believe we are testing you to death. You are not allowed to be kids and play anymore. I'm not really sure we are testing what truly matters, nor can we." It was the only applause I got that day.

Speaking of knowing your ABCs

Do you know your Ps and Qs?

Are you minding your manners?

Are you on your best behavior?

Sometimes we need a subtle—maybe not-so-subtle—reminder of this. The first time I went to Israel, I immediately walked up the information booth and asked, "Can I get a map?"

The volunteer looked at me for a long time and eventually said, "Good Morning." I was ashamed.

After a very, very long and very, very awkward pause, I said: "Good Morning, may I have a map PLEASE?" He smiled as he handed me the map. I had forgotten a few lessons from my childhood—my grandma's constant reminder that "Manners matter," and my mom's constant reminder after receiving a gift: "What do you say?"

I had prepared a few reminders of our retreat for the students. One was a laminated bookmark with the three questions that I start everyday with. Another reminder was a sheet of paper with the numbers 1 to 10 on it to help them begin their "List of 100 Things" they wanted to accomplish. A third was an ABC list, a reminder that knowing your ABC's is not just about singing the alphabet. It is about so much more.

Do you know your ABCs? Think about it!

Think about it with ENTHUSIATICISM! Maybe that word will catch on this time.

Attitudes are contagious is yours worthy of catching?

Bring on a heart attack

Count your routines as blessings and savor life's joys

Discuss a current issue intelligently

Examine a bird's nest with a friend

Focus on people's strengths

Get out of your comfort zone

How interesting you are depends on how interested you are

Invest time and energy for your friends

Jump at the chance to try something new

Keep an open mind and open doors

Leave places better than you found them

Make an impact that will be felt long after you have left

Never stop exploring

Once a moment is gone you can never get it back

Pursue happiness, and catch it

Question Everything

Reach in, reach up, reach out

Solve as much of the puzzle as possible

Today is important. I'm exchanging a day of my life for it

Unplug

Visit wilderness and leave reawakened

We the People means you

eXercise every day

Your uniqueness is irreplaceable

Zero in at what you are good at and become the best at it

# 23. How much would you be worth if you lost all your money?

I am grateful for all of you that have made me a better teacher.

I am grateful for all of you that have made me a better senator.

I am grateful for all of you that have made me a better friend.

I am grateful for all of you that have made me a better husband.

I am grateful for all of you that have made me a better father.

I am grateful for all of you that have made me a better citizen.

I am grateful for all of you that have made me a better human.

Thanksgiving is my favorite holiday, a celebration of bounty and harvest. It is a uniquely American holiday. Watch the Macy's Thanksgiving Day parade and you will have a five-year-old's smile on your face the entire time, although that may be true of any parade.

I love Thanksgiving, Hanukah, Christmas and New Year's. These are times of the year for being thankful, giving back, self-reflection, family and friends, a little holiday cheer, and, well… everything! Oh, and do I have some great holiday jokes.

I loved teaching about the Pilgrims. They had been virtually kicked out of England for their beliefs. They fled to the new world, blazing a trail for millions to follow. Though they had a 50 percent fatality rate, they celebrated life that first autumn. They had no reason to be grateful, yet grateful they were—grateful for their bounty and their freedom. They believed that out of bad comes good, that adversity makes one stronger, and that hard work brings about blessings and benefits. Their most endearing legacy, though, is one we most need to talk about—taking chances and moving forward. They never lost sight of what was truly important in this new land of milk and honey. They never gave up on their American Dream.

Do you know that the Pilgrims left the old world in the spring because they knew April showers would bring Mayflowers to the new world? Do you know why the Pilgrims brought guitars and drums to the new world? They wanted to see Plymouth rock! But I digress.

I repeated the following story before every Thanksgiving break during my entire teaching career.

I woke up one Thanksgiving morning in Chicago. My girlfriend and I were going to go out for dinner to the most expensive and romantic restaurant I could afford. I was going to propose marriage. I wanted to tell her THANKS for all she had done for me, and "Now I want to spend the rest of my life GIVING back to you." Well, this proposing stuff was new to me. I had no idea when and how to do it. What was the protocol here? So, I just came up with my own plan and I was in Chicago on Thanksgiving to execute it.

During dinner, I was a bundle of nerves. I anxiously waited for that perfect moment. While eating, I was looking for the optimal moment. I had checked out a book at the library called *How to Hug*, but when I got home it turned out to be an encyclopedia, so that was not much help. My stomach was in knots. My perplexity was a conundrum of epic proportions. It felt like an oven in that restaurant. Beads of sweat were running down my nose and onto my plate. I wanted to say those simple words, "Will you marry me?" but nothing ever came out.

That night, as I lay in bed, I tried to figure out what had gone wrong? Everything about the evening was perfect, except for my lack of a proposal. *What is wrong with me?* I wondered. *Why could I not pop the question?* After all, that was the whole point of having dinner. I was down, perhaps defeated, but I was not about to quit.

I woke up Friday morning and took my girlfriend to the Chicago Art Institute. As we walked around, I again kept looking for that one magical, romantic painting that would serve as an appropriate backdrop for popping the question... and there it was—a Pissarro, I believe. It showed two young lovers under an umbrella gazing into each other's eyes on the streets of Paris, the most romantic city in the world. It was perfect! As we stood there admiring the masterpiece, I thought, *This is it.* I grabbed her hand and gave her a kiss. Everything was developing perfectly.

That night, as I lay in bed, I again tried to figure out what had gone wrong. Everything was so perfect! *What is wrong with me? Why could I not pop the question?* After all, that was the whole plan. I was down, perhaps defeated, but I was not about to quit.

I woke up on Saturday morning thinking, *OK, today is it!* I was already feeling sick to my stomach. It didn't help that for the last six months, my girlfriend had been leaving suggestive notes around my apartment—notes that said stuff like, "There are a lot of other fish in the sea," and "My biological clock is ticking." Subtle little notes like those.

I thought, *What better place to ask someone to marry you than on top of the tallest building in the world at sunset.* So at dusk, we found ourselves at the top of the Sears Tower—so high we were practically in heaven. It was perfect! We stood there in the western windows gazing at that beautiful orb as it hit the horizon. Mother Nature had never provided a more stunning sunset. As we gazed into each other's eyes and kissed I thought, *This is it!* Everything was so perfect.

That night as I lay in bed, I tried to figure out what had gone wrong? Everything was perfect! *What is wrong with me? Why could I not pop the question?* After all, that was the whole plan. I was down, perhaps defeated, but I was not about to quit.

I woke up on Sunday morning, heartbroken. I wondered what was wrong with me. We were in Chicago for Thanksgiving. I wanted to ask my girlfriend to marry me—to give THANKS for her, and to be GIVING back to her.

On our last day, we went back to the Chicago Art Institute for an hour before catching the train back to Minneapolis. As I frantically searched for an opportunity to propose, I became increasingly discouraged. Eventually, I thought maybe I should just have a guard pass her a note from me saying, "Will you marry me?" But then I thought she might, in desperation, say yes to the guard.

Our trip to Chicago was almost over. The train station stood just blocks away. As we walked out the front door of the Art Institute, I said, "Let's get one last photo of us in Chicago." She stood under the iconic lion statue that majestically guards the Art Institute. I set my camera on the ledge, set the timer, ran into the picture, got on my knees, and said, "Will you marry me?"

The camera clicked.

That photo has been on our mantle for over thirty years now. My only regret is that my wife is standing under the lion's testicles, though some may say it was a fertility metaphor.

One year, after telling this story to my students before Thanksgiving, a student asked, "What do you think took you so long?" If I had been asked that question at any other time, in any other place, at any other moment, I probably would have said, "I don't know." But the stars aligned at that moment of perfect clarity, and the answer came to me in a wave of words. This is what I replied so the entire class could hear it.

Millions of people have asked someone to marry them during a romantic dinner. Millions have asked someone to marry them while standing before a brilliant work of art or architecture. Millions have proposed in front of an amazing display of Mother Nature's creativity. But no one has ever asked someone to marry them under a lion's testicles in front of the Chicago Art Institute—and has a photo of it, to boot!

That is what I was waiting for—a story to tell. Something unique. Oh, and by the way, she said yes! And I've been THANKFUL for her and GIVING to her ever since.

The Pilgrims never gave up, even when facing adversity and misfortune daily. Gratitude and appreciation reigned over them. I love stories like that. Resilience!

Maybe that is the real lesson of my Thanksgiving Proposal story.

My children have had a profound influence on me, as have thousands of my students—not to mention my colleagues, friends, neighbors and my family. In fact, everyone I have met has left an impact on me.

My children have taught me the real meaning behind the expression that we "made good time," which has nothing to do with speed.

My children taught me the real measure of wealth. They made me rich beyond my wildest dreams.

My children improved my spelling. I often asked my wife, "Shall we stop for i-c-e c-r-e-a-m?" or "Where did you hide the d-r-u-m?"

My children taught me to try new things—like bacon ice-cream and macaroni and cheese yogurt. Not to mention passed gas cake.

My children taught me the meaning of humor. When my son was four, he asked us at the dinner table if "The F word is sassy." My wife and I looked at each other and tried not to crack up while wondering which of us would answer. Before either of us spoke, our son curiously shouted out, "You know, FART." My somewhat-knowing eight-year-old cracked up.

My children taught me how to enjoy the holidays. For example, one Halloween they said to me, "Dad, can we do something really scary this Halloween instead of listening to all your Halloween Jokes?"

I said, "Are you sure about that?"

They said, "Yes!" as their mother anxiously looked on.

So, on Halloween, I brought home two baby bunnies, declaring, "Happy Halloween."

The kids looked at me, surprised and perplexed.

"You said you wanted to have a 'hare' raising experience," I reminded them.

One night when my children were about eight and four, my wife and I were having a family squabble during dinner. Suddenly, Erica (the eight-year-old) got up from the table. My wife gave me an embarrassed look that said, "The children are listening to us fight and look at what just happened." No sooner had she finished reprimanding me when the stereo started playing the Beatles song *We Can Work It Out*. My daughter had turned it on. Perfectly timed, the lyrics "Life is very short and there's no time for fussing and fighting, my friend," were coming at us from the stereo—truly a PRICELESS Cwodzinski moment.

Twenty years later, that is the song we played for our father-daughter dance at her wedding.

Our children gave us roots when before that, we only had wings.

They taught us that "staying home tonight" was OK after all.

What are the intangibles you are truly grateful for?

Who are you most thankful for?

Who are you most grateful for?

How much would you be worth if you lost all of your money?

# 24. Do you take for granted boring evenings at home with your family?

A few years ago, I had heard Eli Wiesel speak. During the Q&A, he was asked two questions and I still recall his answers.

The first question was, "Knowing what you know now, if you had a weapon back in 1933 could you have put a bullet in Hitler's head?"

*WOW*! I thought. Wiesel's entire talk had been about peace, love, understanding and forgiveness, and how love conquers hate and violence is never the answer. But I knew he would answer without hesitating, "Of course."

Surprisingly, he replied, "I don't know."

The second question was, "You are known throughout the world as a survivor of the Holocaust, you remain an eminent scholar in your field and you are a Noble Peace Prize Winner. Would you trade it all for the Holocaust to have never happened?"

I know, yes, it seems like a ridiculous question, but his answer was priceless. After a long pause, he looked upward and said, "You mean I could have dinner with my sister tonight?"

Never take for granted a boring evening at home with your family.

The program ended and I was planning to jump on the stage, give him a hug and tell him, "My life will never be the same, thank you," but he was whisked off the stage. Along with everyone else, I walked out. But I knew the building backward and forward because in my college days, I had ushered there, so I decided to go where I thought Wiesel would be going to greet local political and business leaders. I crept up the stairs leading to a side banquet room with a sign reading, "Private Event Do Not Enter!" I cracked open the door and observed numerous people in suits and dresses, but Wiesel was nowhere in sight. I was in shorts and a T-shirt, so clearly I'd get busted as soon as I entered the room, so I walked down the steps and turned around.

There, standing alone in a side room, was Eli Wiesel. Suddenly, he and I were alone together. For the first time in my life, I was star struck—speechless. Dumbstruck! I was in front of my idol, my hero, and I could not think of anything to say. There I was, one-on-one with perhaps the greatest philosopher of my lifetime, and both of us were just staring at each other.

Finally, I made my arm move. I stuck it out and shook his hand for what seemed like an eternity. I must have said, "Thank you!" twenty times in those few seconds. Then, being respectful of his time, I left the room. As I retreated, I wondered why he was alone and not mingling with all the bigwigs in the reception area. I guess I'll never know.

I loved taking my students to Arlington National Cemetery first thing in the morning and then spending the afternoon at the Holocaust Museum. It had become a DC tradition and always produced an emotional rollercoaster of a day. One year, after exploring Arlington, we were heading to The Holocaust Museum with a few inspirational stops along the way when one of my students began sobbing. She had lost her camera. I told her that there is no way we could retrace the morning's steps, but there were over thirty students who have the same pictures on their cameras.

We were behind schedule, so I started marching toward the exit when she pleaded, "Is there nothing we can do?"

I replied that we could report her loss at the visitor center. I knew this would make her a little happier but doubted that the camera would ever be found.

We were getting further behind schedule when one of the other students suggested that he could run back and try to find her camera—a rare act of chivalry.

I told him no. Our route entailed crossing freeways and winding paths and heading up a hill and then through a field. He would never find us.

Begrudgingly, he agreed and we started marching. Less than a minute later, he approached again, got on his knees and begged me to let him run back to find the camera. This time I looked at him, pointed out three cross country runners in our group, and told them they could all go if they stuck together. This was before cell phones and MapQuest, so I asked them to memorize our route. They did, and I let them go.

Thirty minutes later, as we were heading up the hill to the Iwo Jima Memorial, our four young heroes raced up to me, one of them triumphantly holding the camera over his head. I thought, *Chivalry apparently is not dead, and that is one impressive young man.* Cheers erupted and smiles abounded. The girl, joyous and grateful, finally stopped crying.

Four hours later, we were winding down our visit through the Holocaust Museum. This was the only venue where, before entering, I told the students, "If you have any questions as we go through the museum, remember them or write them down, then ask me after we leave." I was standing in the Hall of Remembrance, ready to light a candle for my ancestors who were murdered, when the girl who had lost and recovered her camera came up to me in tears.

*What could be wrong now?* I wondered. She held up her precious camera and said in a barely audible voice, "I've never been more ashamed in my life to make a fuss over such a small thing," No more words were needed. In this hallowed space honoring millions of tortured souls, we both knew exactly what she meant. I gave her a hug and said, "We've all grown up a lot today, haven't we?"

She nodded knowingly.

The angriest I've ever been at a student occurred when we were leaving the Holocaust Museum. A student suddenly proclaimed, "I'm starving." The other chaperone looked at me and with a feces-eating smile, knowing fireworks were about to go off. The chaperone knew that the last thing you'd ever want Cwod to hear while you were leaving the Holocaust Museum was, "I'm starving."

I waited a few second, hoping the young man would realize how insensitive, tactless and thoughtless his comment was, but instead, he rejoiced at seeing a nearby hot dog stand. I pounced. "Don't you realize where you just were? That millions starved death in the death camps? That millions were murdered there? Don't you need some time to digest all that?" He walked past the hot dog stand... and rapidly away from me.

I met a Holocaust survivor who told me that her grandchildren would say, "I'll just die if I don't get that thing I want." After a long sigh, she said, "Steven, when they say that, I never know whether to laugh or cry."

Next time you are bored sitting in your living room or at the kitchen table, take pause. Reflect on all the intangibles around you.

I'm not sure if there are ghosts or spirits among us, or the souls of previous lives. But I do know this. I was at the Maidanek death camp in Poland reflecting on the horrors of humanity among the ruins when I came upon a barracks lit by one bare light bulb. My eyes were still adjusting to the low light when I felt a breeze behind me. The hair stood up on my back. I quickly turned around, but no one was there—I was all alone. After my eyes adjusted, I saw that the room was filled with the shoes left behind by those who were murdered. A young child's white dress shoes caught my eye, and I experienced something as close to a spiritual moment as I'd ever had. It was as if all those murdered Jews were watching over their shoes. Haunted? That is not the right word, but I can't think of a better one to describe what had happened to me in that sacred place.

I have studied the Holocaust extensively. I've been to most of the major death camps in Eastern Europe, met dozens of survivors and read dozens of books. I enjoyed teaching the stories of the Holocaust more than anything else. I would communicate the statistics, the historical record, the photos—the sheer magnitude of it all. Then I would shift gears and tell my students what I really wanted them to learn.

During my lecture, I would hold up my tattered copy of Victor Frankl's *Man's Search for Meaning*. I'd tell my students Frankl's great epiphanies, that "Everything can be taken from a person but the freedom of choosing one's attitude," and "Having meaning in life is not as vital as having meaning in the moment." Then I would hold up a copy of Anne Frank's diary and ask, "What might have been? What if?"

I would do this to help them understand that the meaning of our very existence is to leave the world better than we found it. To cause them to comprehend that we can set out to leave this universe grander than when we came upon it. To get them to realize we can all make a wonderful impact that will be felt long after we are gone.

And yes, to help them NEVER take for granted a boring evening at home with our family.

# 25. How much smiling and laughing have you done today?

It is healthier to smile, laugh and grin than to frown, yell and scowl.

I was very strict during my first few years in the classroom. I belonged to the "Never let the students see you smile or laugh until Christmas" fraternity of teachers. If you let your guard down, for even a minute, I believed it could take days to regain discipline and control.

One year, after a good friend of mine retired from teaching. I asked, if he could go back and change one thing in his career, what would it be? He replied, "I would have relaxed and had more fun." Sound advice, indeed.

Early in my career, a kid in the hallway, that I had had in class was screwing around, so I told him to "Knock it off." He looked up at me and yelled, "Get f*cked!" I went to the principal's office intending to have him placed in detention, or suspended, or even expelled. Such a serious breach of authority required a serious consequence!

I told the principal a student had told me to get f*cked. After a long pause, and with a slightly devilish smirk, he replied, "How was it"?

I stormed out of his office, angrier than when I went in and got about thirty feet down the hall when I stopped dead in my tracks and cracked up. I thought, *Now that is funny*. The principal had put the incident into perspective for me, conveying to his new, uptight teacher that this was not the end of the world, and quite frankly not that big of a deal.

I'm so grateful to that principal for reminding me of the power of humor to help us lighten up and put things in perspective. Ever since, when I hear kids swearing at someone in the hall, I ask them to "Please find a more intelligent and articulate way to express your dissatisfaction with another member of your species."

Laughing brings oxygen into our system, improving our mood. When we laugh, we take deeper breaths, increasing the blood flow to our vital organs and brain. Thus, we become more creative and more engaged, we learn better and faster. We add joy and zest to our life, easing our anxiety, stress and fear.

When we experience a good laugh, our brain secretes endorphins, which are the "feel-good" brain chemicals that elevate mood and improve the ability to cope. The movement caused by laughter actually exercises many muscles of the body. Laughter research has shown that humor helps to keep the body strong and disease-resistant.

When was the last time you laughed until it hurt? Or you slapped your knee?

If you could do anything right now that would make you smile or laugh, what would it be?

In your circle of friends, who makes you laugh the hardest?

Think of someone you know who has died. Can you remember their laugh?

How does laughing make you feel?

Laugh at yourself.

Attempt to laugh at circumstances rather than griping about them.

Surround yourself with reminders to lighten up and keep things in perspective.

I truly believe I learned more from my students than I ever taught them. For instance, I learned to never let a teenage boy randomly pick a number between 1 and 100. Here are some of the other lessons I learned from my students.

## Humility

Some of the most challenging experiences of my teaching career involved trying to live the adage of never giving up on our species.

Some of those experiences (OK, most of them) involved faux pas of my own making. Many moments were humbling and embarrassing. They did, however, crack me up, or make me think, or make me a better person—like the time I told the student who was going blind that "Your story was a real eye-opener for me."

## Cwod

My students call me "Cwod." During my first few years teaching, I would put students into detention for calling me "Cwod" rather than the formal "Mr. Cwodzinski." I thought calling me the more casual nickname was a sign of disrespect—or worse, that my students were being too chummy with me.

"You need to call me Mr. Cwodzinski," I'd tell them as I made them stay after school. *That will teach them*, I thought. Then one day, as I was hauling a kid down to detention, he boldly asked me, "Why are you sending me to restricted study?"

I explained, "Because you disrespected me. You called me Cwod."

"But everyone calls you Cwod."

He was right, so I had to say, "OK then, you can go."

As he walked away, he looked back and said, "We call you Cwod because we love your class. It's a sign of endearment, not to mention it's a heck of a lot easier to pronounce."

To all the students I put in restricted study before I realized calling me Cwod was ok, I'm sorry.

## One A-

I ran into an ex-student the summer after he graduated. I knew he had almost been Valedictorian but had just missed a 4.0 GPA. I asked him how close had he come? He said he had earned all As, except for one A-.

"Bummer," I said. "In which class did you get an A-?"

He said he couldn't remember.

"Come on," I coaxed, "you must remember the mean teacher that ruined your perfect record?"

He looked at me and smiled. "OK, it was you."

He had not wanted to hurt my feelings. That was one fine young man—mature beyond his years.

## Exploding Coffee Cup

In class one day, I started answering a question that got me all excited but forgot I was holding a full cup of coffee. As I flailed my arms, I threw the cup onto the floor at Mach speed. The cup smashed and the coffee went flying—not in a 360-degree spread like you'd think, but straight up, drenching me in hot coffee. The splash defied the laws of physics.

The students started howling, but I never stopped my enthusiastic and witty answer to the student's question. The students stopped laughing and took on concerned looks as if questioning whether I realized what had just happened. I loved it and eventually cracking up, though I do recall that my shirt and pants were ruined.

## Conferences

At a parent-teacher conference, one parent showed up on crutches. She said she had sprained her ankle after taking up running. I said to this rather large mom, "You'll have to find another way to lose weight." She was not impressed.

At another conference, a frazzled parent looked down at her feet and began laughing so hard she almost cried. So, I looked down at her feet too. She was wearing bunny slippers. I cracked up as well, though I was a little concerned.

## Genital

At yet a different conference, a mom said, "Why do you call my daughter 'Genital?'"

The color must have drained from my face as I asked, "What"?

Suddenly laughing, she said that one of her daughter's male foreign friends, who was also in my class, had recently come to dinner and asked, "Why does Mr. Cwodzinski call you Genital." The friend was learning English—it was not his first language. He had thought I was saying "Genital" when I called on "Chantelle." The mother could not have been more cool about it.

I suppose I could have annunciated better.

## The Twins

During the third week of class, I was lecturing about China's one-child policy. A girl's hand went up, and she asked, "What if you are a twin?"

I said, "Great question. Are you a twin?"

"Are you kidding me?" she said, pointing out the look-alike girl right next to her wearing the same dance team outfit. "We're identical twins!"

By the end of the third week, I suppose I could have been more observant.

## Debate

I was the debate coach for the high school. When we showed up for our first big tournament, I was nervous and excited, as were my students. We had prepared for weeks on the topic of "Capital Punishment." My team was prepared and ready to go. My students went to their respective rooms to begin debating, but within minutes began filtering back to where we were supposed to meet after the round.

I asked, "Why are you done so soon?"

The students seemed upset. (See, sometimes I can be observant.) I said, "What's wrong?"

They shot back, "We're supposed to be debating Affirmative Action. You prepared us for the wrong topic!" (I'm not going to mention the time I drove to the wrong high school.)

I suppose I could have been more observant of the debate schedule.

## Shoes

One day, I inadvertently wore two different-colored shoes with two different heel sizes to school. Halfway through the day, a student asked me, "Why are you wearing shoes with different colors today?" I looked down at my feet. I had made it through first hour and homeroom without noticing. Nor had the scores of students and staff I had encountered pointed out my wardrobe malfunction—though I'm sure they were laughing at my expense.

I suppose I could have been more observant by the beginning of third hour.

## Zipper

One year I was discussing the artist Robert Mapplethorpe. We were debating the National Endowment for the Arts. It was a lesson most definitely for mature students. Raising questions like "What is art?" and "Is obscenity protected under the First Amendment?" I had given this same lesson for years with the students being mature, respectful, and interested. However, one year, kids started giggling and whispering as I went through a few more "obscene" works of art. At first, I blew them off and kept plowing through. Eventually I lost it, pointing at the kid laughing the hardest, I yelled "What is so funny?" He replied, "We are all trying to decide who should tell you your pants are unzipped." There is never a good way for a teacher to handle that one. Of course, it had to happen during a discussion about controversial art of a sexual nature. That summer I ran into the student and his mom at the mall. She said to me, "My son told me about some of your antics." I was too taken aback to comment. A few years later, every teachers' worst nightmare occurred again. The bell rang, and the students walked out of the room. Sitting on my podium was a very nice, polite, note containing a smiley face. I opened the note. It said: Your pants are unzipped.

## Second Place

A student, one of my all-time favorites, was crying in the hallway. I said, "What is wrong?" She said, "I came in second place in the tournament." Recently she had come in second place as home coming queen and second place in a contest in my class. I thought, *What I can say to this young woman who is crying all alone and sitting on the floor in the hallway after school in order to comfort her?*

So, I said, "You know, you are one of those people that will always come in second place." What a huge compliment, I thought. To always come in second place, wow!

She looked up at me with a look that screamed "WHAT, are you nuts? Is that supposed to make me feel better?" I did not think anything of it until the next day when I started telling a few of my peers about the student and what I had said. They looked at me like I was out of my mind. "You said what, you insensitive bastard" seemed to be the most recurring comment. I tried to tell them that I thought it was a huge compliment. My peers simply shook their heads and could not believe I had said such an insensitive thing to someone who was so distraught. Later when I polled my classes, only one student sided with me.

## Unabomber

We had one computer for a department of 16 that had access to the internet, it was in the social studies resource room. It was the day the New York Times released the Unabomber manuscript. I sat down with our department secretary to find the on-line manuscript, so I could print it. I was very excited for this new experience. It was to be the first time I ever searched the internet. The secretary booted up the internet and said, "Type in here what you are searching for." So, I typed in "Unabomber", and anxiously awaited the result. Up on the screen popped up a full-frontal nude woman. I reached under the desk and pulled out every cord I could reach, shutting down the computer. I turned around to see if any students were behind me watching what we were doing. None had seen the search results, I breathed a sigh of relief. When I asked my students what happened they said the system probably thought you searched "bombshell."

## Tommorow

During my entire student teaching assignment, I left written on the chalkboard: "<u>Tommorow's Assignment</u>." Beneath those words, I would write the assignment due the next day. When my nine weeks were done, I met with my supervising teacher and my student teaching supervisor. I asked them, "How do you think I did?

They said, "You're among the best student teachers we've ever worked with, but there's just one thing. You need to learn how to spell 'Tomorrow.'" It had been misspelled on the chalkboard, the entire term, and the kids knew it.

I suppose I could have been more observant during those nine weeks.

150

## Resent

After email had arrived on the scene, a parent agreed to forward a group email for me. I sent her my original message about an upcoming DC trip. She replied, "I resent your last message."

I had no idea what had upset her about the message but was worried I had somehow hurt her feelings. I went to a counselor and asked her to read the email and tell me what was so offensive that the parent had "resented" it.

She laughed and said, "Cwod, she 're-sent' your message to the people in the group. She did not 'resent' your message."

I could never have been an English teacher.

## Spellcheck

After spellcheck was introduced, I over- relied on it when I added the following questions to an assignment:

What president was confined to a wheelbarrow? (wheelchair)

What was Clinton's pubic policy? (public)

The students thought I was trying to be funny. I wasn't (not that time, anyway.)

Shortly after that, I sent out an email to parents and let spellcheck to its magic again. I signed the email 'Cwod,' but spellcheck changed it to 'Clod.' Some of those parents probably thought it was no error.

## Grooming

During my team-teaching days, I was teamed with a woman who stopped by my room one day to address our students about some matter. We were standing together when she noticed a hair on my shirt and thoughtfully tried to pull it off. Unbeknownst to her, that hair was attached to my body, having worked its way through the fabric. When she realized it was still attached to my chest, she let out the loudest scream I've ever heard, and then made a series of gestures suggesting how totally grossed out and mortified she was. I was so embarrassed! But boy, did I laugh. Not nearly as hard as the students did, though.

## Atomic Red Hot

As I was lecturing one day, a student set down a bag of Atomic Red Hots on her desk. I grabbed one and threw it into my mouth without missing a beat of my lecture. A few moments later, I swallowed the Red Hot by accident and it got stuck in my throat. I stopped lecturing and tried to swallow it. When I couldn't swallow it, I tried to cough it up, but that did not work either.

By this time, my lecture had been paused for about thirty, maybe forty seconds. My students were bewildered. Then I motioned with my hands that I was choking—and my class cracked up. It was now closing in on a minute, and my throat was on fire, so I ran to the classroom across the hall and gestured that I was choking. That cracked them up too. *That's the guy who is always telling jokes and screwing around*, everyone thought.

Meanwhile, one of my own students must have realized that I was, in fact, choking and had called the nurse. Within seconds, the nurse was coming at me about forty miles an hour to deliver the Heimlich Maneuver. And then suddenly I swallowed it.

As a result of the obstruction and the burning, I could not talk for three days. My wife and my students were extremely happy.

## Boo-Boo

I made plenty of mistakes during my career. I once had a student who happened to be a ghost. His parents had signed up for conferences but never showed up. When I said something to the young ghost the next day, he said, "My parents were there, but you blew them off."

"I never saw them," I said, surprised.

"Of course you didn't," he said. "They're 'trans-parents.'" He later told me he was a mistake.

"What?" I said.

He told me that his ghost parents had not take proper precautions during a moment of intimacy, and the result was a little Boo-Boo. But, I digress.

These are just a few of the many lessons I learned in the classroom. Eat a little humble pie from time to time and laugh at yourself once in a while—or in my case, every day. It tastes good.

I wish I could say I have a clear record as a state senator but...

## A Smashing Debut

On my first day on the floor of the Senate chambers, I made a smashing debut. We had just installed glass desktop covers to preserve the original desks in the hundred-year-old restored chamber. Someone had failed to secure the glass. I had been sitting at my desk for a few moments when a colleague came to talk to me and the glass desktop cover slowly slid off and shattered, sending shards in every direction and reverberating throughout the chamber. That was my smashing debut on the Senate floor.

## Shirt

I had met a conservative lobbyist for breakfast and he wanted to discuss ways we could reach across the aisle in the coming session. As we left our hour-long meeting, he said, "Are you going anywhere important now?"

I replied "Yes, I'm meeting some constituents."

"You may want to turn your shirt right side out," he advised, "because it's currently inside out." Boy did we laugh. You see, we can all get along if we just care a little about each other.

What is your most embarrassing moment that makes you laugh now?

Have you had more smiling and laughing today than you had frowning and yelling?

# 26. How do you pursue happiness?

Iused a great deal of humor in my classroom. I believe that HAHAHA moments will get you quicker to an AHA! moment. (Of course, I did not start my career this way.)

I told jokes before exams, and I placed jokes throughout my exams to lower test anxiety. My students usually just moaned and groaned when they heard or read my jokes—some booed, some laughed, but everyone smiled with me or at me. Most were more appropriate for second graders than for seniors. At the very least, I cracked up at the looks of utter disbelief on their faces.

One time, on a grant application, I wrote, "I tell jokes before a test to lower their test anxiety. Students moan because they are so stupid." I had meant the jokes were stupid, not the students. I did not receive the grant.

The first time I told jokes before a test, no one laughed. When I got home that night, I threw the jokes into the fire. At least the fire roared.

When no one would laugh at my jokes, I would call the material "college level" and tell students, "You guys are just not ready for this type of intellectual humor." One kid in the class would always reply, "Your jokes are just not funny." Buzz kill!

After one particularly bad joke, a student shouted, "That joke is so old!"

"Old jokes never die," I said. "They just sound that way." And then added, "I hope you live to be as old as that joke."

One of my classic jokes is one I use when I showed up late to an event. "With a very serious expression, I would say, "Sorry I am late, but I was at the mall and the power went out. I was stuck on the escalator for twenty minutes." Whoever was listening either laughed or asked, "Don't you mean the elevator?" Some simply wondered why I didn't just walk up or down the escalator when the power went out. Nevertheless, I cracked up at their responses.

If I would see a student struggling with a test question, I sometimes handed them a rubber band and told them to wrap it around their head. That it would help them make "snap decisions."

Here's an example of how I would sneak some humor into a test.

16. Where can the amendments to the Constitution be found?
   a. In the preamble to the Constitution
   b. In the "unwritten Constitution"
   c. After Article VII of the Constitution
   d. In the last place you look

Now you can see why my students just groaned. Occasionally, during an exam, a kid would belly laugh, I would say "Question 16?". That student would smile and nod with delight.

Avoid having quotidian days! No day should be routine, common or normal. There simply are not enough days in our lives.

It seems obvious that when we laugh, we are happy, and when we are happy we are more productive, and when we are more productive, well......

When I was a young man, I told my mother that I hoped someday to marry a woman who could take a joke.

"What other kind do you think you will get?" she replied.

Humor and laughter are not just about having fun and telling jokes and partying. It's a way of seeing the world.

I asked a girl out in junior high. "Don't make me laugh," she said. We did not see the world in the same way.

My teachers used to tell me back in school to "wipe that smile off your face." I thought that was a ridiculous thing to tell someone. Don't make me laugh and stop being so happy? Indeed! What was wrong with these people?

155

I tried to fill each day with a little bit of buffoonery, whimsy, shenanigans, pranks and tomfoolery—often at my own expense. Like the time two of my colleagues came into my classroom in spandex uniforms as Tabula and Rosa carrying a bucket of water, a sponge and a leaf blower. My blackboard was covered with lecture notes. They proceeded to cleanse and dry it, leaving a blank slate. I wish I had a video of that—it would have gone viral.

One time I was walking through the halls as our school was undergoing a massive construction project. It was a real mess. I came upon a fellow teacher who had been raised in Nazi Germany. She was excited and screaming joyously, assuming I would share in her enthusiasm.

"Steven, they just tore down the wall!" she said.

I nodded, telling her, "That's great!" and just walked away. I wondered, though, which wall come down that would have brought about in my colleague such rapture.

I walked into the front office and asked the secretary what wall that might have caused such excitement.

The secretary gave me a strange look and said, "Cwod, the Berlin Wall is coming down."

I did an about-face and ran back to the German teacher telling her how happy I was for her nation of birth to be reunited. I gave her a big hug and told her why I had blown her off. We laughed for years over that.

Now, as a state senator, I go into classrooms to talk about history and government. Someone always asks me what I miss most about teaching. I usually tell them how much fun I had with my students and my colleagues.

"I once had a 'foreign exchange' student from Hawaii." Every time I began this story for our students, I would pause and look at their faces for a reaction. Only a few would get it. Then I'd continue:

"She never laughed at my jokes, so one day I kept her after class. I asked her 'So how do you like being here in the United States?' She looked at me kind of funny. Then I asked her what she thought of my jokes.

"She said: 'They're hilarious!' I asked her why she never laughed at them. She replied 'I'm a Hawaiian.'

"'So?' I asked, and she said, 'We laugh with A-lo-ha.'

"I smiled and added, 'Well in Minnesota. we laugh with a Minnie-ha-ha.'"

OK, I never had a foreign exchange student from Hawaii. But I digress.

Oh, and before I forget, always carry a joke or two around with you in your pocket. You may make a friend smile who is sad or be the life of the party.

Once, my college-age son said to me, "We have this game we play where we name a music group and we all say our favorite song." I told him we use to call that game a conversation.

My students would often ask me about my favorite film or song or book. I would then have to discuss SET and SETTING. What is your mindset at this very moment? Are you feeling melancholic and mellow? Are you feeling joyful and jubilant? What is your state of mind? What is the physical setting you are in?

It is hard to say, for example, what your favorite song is to get the pedal to the metal, to dance to, to sing along with, to be inspired by, or for its impact on society, or to reflect upon. It all depends, doesn't?

My top ten lists change depending on my set and setting. The items on our national Top Ten lists change through the seasons and the decades. But here is a list as of this moment. If a list can indeed change your life, here is one that is in no particular order, that may Shake Your Spirit and Stir Your Soul!—changing how you think about and see the world.

## My Favorite Ten Albums

The Beatles *Abbey Road* (well actually all of the Beatles albums)
Lou Reed's *Transformer*
Nillson's *Nillson Schmillson*
CSNY's *Déjà vu*
Pink Floyd's *Dark Side of the Moon*
The Pretender's *The Pretenders*
America's *America*

Eagles *Desperado*
Spirit's *Twelve Dreams of Doctor Sardonicus*
Cat Steven's *Tea for the Tillerman*

## My Favorite Ten Books

Vonnegut's *Slaughterhouse Five*
Frankl's *Man's Search for Meaning*
Bryson's *Walk in the Woods*
Orwell's *1984*
Weiner's *Geography of Bliss*
Kennedy Toole's *Confederacy of Dunces*
Silverstein's *The Giving Tree*
Heller's *Catch 22*
Clarke's *The Last Campaign*
Dawidowicz's *War Against the Jews*

## My Favorite Ten Songs

The Beatles *We Can Work It Out* or *Hey Jude* (I get two Beatles songs)
The Rolling Stones *You Can't Always Get What You Want*
Simon and Garfunkel's *Bridge Over Troubled Waters*
Donovan's *Atlantis*
Bob Marley *Three Little Birds*
Cat Stevens *Miles From Nowhere*
Beach Boys *And I Kissed Her*
U2 *Pride*
Dylan *Like a Rolling Stone*
Jackson Browne's *Your Bright Baby Blue*

## My Favorite Ten Films

*Life is Beautiful*
*City Lights*
*Schindler's List*
*Mr. Smith Goes to Washington*
*Field of Dreams*
*It's a Wonderful Life*

*Saving Private Ryan*
*Miracle on 34th Street*
*Harold and Maude*
*Citizen Kane*

## My Favorite Ten Paintings

Baskakov's *Milkmaids*
Rembrandt's *The Night Watch*
Sargent's *Gassed*
Rivera's *Detroit Industry Murals*
Rockwell's *Four Freedoms*
David's *Death of Socrates*
Bierstadt's *Among the Sierra Nevada*
Cole's *Voyage of Life*
Bosch's *Garden of Earthly Delights*
Wyeth's *Christina's World*

Make a Top Ten list of your favorite albums, sports moments, paintings, songs, cities, trails or books. You can make a Top Ten list for just about anything.

Have your friends all bring a Top Ten list without their names on it to your next social gathering. Pass out enough copies for everyone.

Guess who each list belongs to.

Maybe this will become the next new parlor game.

Let the conversations begin!

What are on your Top Ten lists?

What Shakes Your Spirit and Stirs Your Soul?

What brings you joy?

The United States of America guarantees each of us the pursuit of happiness. We the people, however, have to catch it. Have Fun!

# 27. Do you belong to something bigger than yourself?

I team-taught a "Block" class for over ten years with another teacher. We combined American history with American literature and gave each section a cute adorable name so we could differentiate one class from the other: Aardvarks, Badgers, Chinchillas, Dolphins, Egrets, and F. As I write this, I cannot for the life of me remember the F class animal. I'm sure I will hear from the original members of that class. It was fun going through all the animals and trying to avoid sexual innuendos or other inappropriate metaphors. When my colleague suggested Beavers and Cougars, I had to explain that they may not be a good idea.

My colleague and I believed it was a way to make our huge school a little smaller as well as encourage the students to belong to something bigger than themselves. The collective sum of our parts is so much greater. The whole is almost always greater than the sum of its parts.

My team-teaching class morphed into a political science class, so we adopted different names: Activists, Bi-partisans, Constituents, Delegates, Electorates, and Federalists. Cute, right? This time, the Block concept was an AP American Government class combined with an AP Comparative Government class.

The students really felt like they were part of something bigger. They would proudly proclaim "I am a Dolphin" or "I am an Activist."

Ten years later I still I run into ex-students who remember being an Aardvark or a Falcon (I remember what F stood for now).

We taught at a high school with over 3,500 students. I thought that giving each class a cute name would make the school seem a little bit smaller, and it did. We were a family. We had picnics, film nights, talent shows, book clubs and seminars. It was a great concept for a course. I taught that the purpose of our program was so much more than just content and curriculum.

I was fortunate to teach "The Block" for a number of years and "APPS" after that, which consisted of some highly enthusiastic and civic-minded young people. On the last day of our APPS class, we gathered all the students for a final celebration and ended the course with a tantalizing statement: "Ask us anything you want." My fellow APPS teacher and I got such wonderful questions:

To what degree did you control the course of your life?
What is your greatest mistake and what did you learn from it?
What would you title your autobiography?
Which of your qualities are you most proud of?

God, I Loved Teaching!

Our school had a clothing drive as well as a food drive every year. "The Block" became infamous for bringing in more items than the rest of the school combined. Every year, we shattered the previous school record. The school record for all 3,500 students had been 11,000 items, and the "Block" (with just 180 students) brought in 13,000 items. Another year, "The Block" brought in 12,523 items of clothing, out of the school's total of: 15,719 items. I was so very proud.

When colleagues and parents and community members asked how we did that, I would simply say: "I have amazing parents who bring to me some amazing kids, and I try to create an environment where the students feel like they are part of something bigger than themselves. A family of one hundred eighty kids in a school of 3,500 students.

One of my most unforgettable stories involves the High School Food Drive. It was during one of my first years of teaching and the principal made the following statement during morning announcements:

"Well done, Mr. or Ms. so and so's first hour. You won the food drive today by bringing in thirty-six cans. Second place is Mr. so and so's class with twenty-two items, and coming in at third was Ms. so and so's class with seven items. Tomorrow, Mr. so and so's first hour will get donuts for a job well done. So, students, come on—you can do better than that. The drive ends on Friday."

I participated for the next few years. On Monday, the staff and I would pump up the first hour classes to bring in cans for the food drive. Mondays, year after year, brought in the same results, the winning first hour having brought in something like forty-three items, thus getting donuts the following day. By the end of the week, first hours were bringing in hundreds of items as more and more students began to participate, so that by Friday, to get donuts, the first hour had to bring in over five hundred items. But it worked, and the local food shelves were very grateful.

One year, though, I had an epiphany. While the staff was beginning to pump up the classes on Monday, I started pumping them up the Thursday and Friday of the previous week. For years, my strategy worked. The previous week I would tell my first hour to "bring in cans, bring in cans, bring in cans" on Monday. My first hour won every single year by bringing in all their food on Monday. Most of the staff would not jump on the bandwagon until Tuesday or even Wednesday. They never had a chance.

When the principal would get on the microphone at the end of Monday, he would always announce Mr. Cwodzinski's first hour brought in 6,456 items… and in second place is Ms. so and so's class with forty-one. For years, this was great. We got donuts every Tuesday, but more importantly, we raised the bar for the entire week—and local food shelves benefitted.

Then arrived a most memorable year. The previous week I had been really motivating students to "bring in cans" for the drive, and everyone was very excited. When Monday arrived, my first hour shattered every record for a food drive. One group brought their items to class on a toboggan. Cans were piled high in the front of the class. When the bell rang, I was standing in front of (some might say buried in) a huge mound of food. It was more comfortable being buried in the clothing drive than the food drive.

As I was busting with pride for a job well done, I was also scanning the class to see who was absent. I noticed an ESL (English as Second Language) student was oddly missing. He was never absent and always highly focused, his body language stating clearly: "Do not call on me, please, I just want to learn about American government and work on my English. I choose to be anonymous." That morning, for the first time, he was absent. I was concerned for him.

But I was proud of my fine young students. At this point, about a minute after the bell rang, the door flew open. An interesting point: When students are late to class, they open the door one of two ways— quietly and nervously with an embarrassed expression, which said, "I am so sorry" and "Please do not call my house." The other is loud, brash, obnoxious, and boisterous, which screamed "here I am everybody, take notice". In this case, he opened my door the latter way, so I looked and there was the ESL student with a broad smile that would have melted any mother's heart. Over his shoulder was slung a green garbage bag filled with empty pop cans for what I can only assume he thought was a recycling can drive. I'm sure he expected to bring in the largest number of cans and be the class hero. He had heard me saying, "Bring in cans, bring in cans, bring in cans."

When he saw that his presumed recycling can drive was, in fact, a food can drive, his beaming expression turned south. His expression would have broken any mother's heart. I told the new student, "That's great, we can use all the empty pop cans from the recycling bins this week, and when we get cash for them, we can give that cash to the food shelves. What a great idea! I'm surprised no one had thought of that before—well done!" The smile returned to his face. I told him to take his cans to the lunch room and I'd have custodians save all the pop cans for the week. He turned and walked away a very proud young man.

The door had not been shut behind the student for ten seconds when my class erupted in laughter. I let them enjoy themselves for a moment. After the laughter had died down, I explained that a lifetime of making mistakes was more honorable than a lifetime spent doing nothing. That quiet kid walking to the lunchroom had finally reached out to say, "Notice me, I want to help make a difference, I want to make friends." The students could have scarred that kid for the rest of his life if they had laughed at him to his face.

"I don't know who I am prouder of right now," I told the students, "him for wanting to make a difference, or all of you for being sensitive enough to understand his emotions and not humiliate him." I ended by saying, "Remember we might not always be doing the right thing, but we must always be doing something."

Teachable Moments! Lessons not found in the lesson plan.

A student once said to me, "We miss being in a class that we really take pride in." Pride: the feeling of being a part of something bigger than oneself—that you are accomplishing something you alone cannot do."

Two boy scouts came to my house one day asking if I would like to make a donation for the new community swimming pool. I gave them two gallons of water. But I digress.

Belong to something bigger than yourself. Yes, indeed!

# 28. Have you earned this?

One day, my son said, "I don't have to pick up my crayons." He proudly stated his rationale with his hands on his hips: "It's a free country."

I explained that we all have obligations and responsibilities as Americans. We have to toil and leave this place better than when we found it. "So, you need to pick up your crayons," I said. This is your duty, it is your civic duty." I told him that JFK had declared: "Ask not what your country can do for you; ask what you can do for your country."

My point was that this isn't a free country. It was far from free. Freedom is not free! There have been far too many sacrifices. There are and will be many more future sacrifices required to improve upon a near-perfect union, which our forefathers and foremothers gave us. By this time, five minutes into my tirade, my son had long ago picked up his crayons and disappeared.

As parents, we have all heard far too often the cries:

"It's a free country."

"You cannot tell me what to do."

"You can't make me."

God knows. I had heard it as a teacher!

On the first day of class, I always asked my students if they could name all five members of the Simpson Family. They came up with the names within seconds. Then I would ask if they could name the five fundamental freedoms found in the First Amendment. This question took them a little longer. Most could name two, or perhaps three. One year, to justify why they could name all the Simpsons but didn't know the five freedoms, a student said, "The Simpsons have been on for like twenty years." The fact that the Bill of Rights was over two hundred years old seemed to have been missed.

Hennepin County, in which I taught, has a series of "defenses" for teens who are out past curfew. My favorite is: "It is an affirmative defense for a juvenile to prove that they were exercising First Amendment rights protected by the United States Constitution…"

I loved that you can be out past curfew if you are exercising your First Amendment rights. What a country! Although I should say, what a county! When I lecture on freedom of speech, I usually discuss Texas V. Johnson, which made categorized flag-burning as protected speech.

I kept a little 4 x 6 inch American flag and a cigarette lighter in my classroom and told my students that when both of my kids got their drivers licenses, they had hoped for a car. Instead they both got a handheld US flag and a lighter, like the one I held up. I told my kids to keep the flags and lighter in the glovebox. If they ever got pulled over after curfew, they were told to simply jump out of the car, light the flag on fire and begin chanting: "US out of Iraq." I could tell some of my students were thinking "I need to do that." In fact, I believe a few did.

One day a student came to my class wearing a very offensive T-shirt. OK, it actually happened a few times over the years. I asked this student if she thought the message on her shirt was offensive to anyone.

She immediately shot back, "What about my rights?"

I respectfully responded, "What about your responsibilities?"

"What?"

I repeated the question.

She said "Huh?"

At that moment, I had an epiphany. We all scream, "WHAT ABOUT MY RIGHTS?" yet how often do we ever scream "WHAT ABOUT MY RESPONSIBIILTIES?" Given any controversial situation, we immediately demand to exercise our rights. But do we ever wonder what our responsibilities are?

I remember a huge fight that occurred at our high school. Kids were cheering and yelling for different sides, and it was total chaos. The fight was finally broken up, and we eventually got the kids back into their classes. When the seniors were sitting down, they—OK, it was just the boys—were all fired up. Testosterone filled the air.

Suddenly, a foreign exchange student raised his hand and asked, "What is my role as a senior when a fight breaks out in the school?"

The class fell silent. I did not say a word, just let the question sink in for a moment. What is my role indeed, SENIORS! The students, I think, were ashamed of their behavior. It had taken a question from a foreign exchange student from Japan to help them realize it. It was one of those "teachable moments" where my silence spoke volumes. Sometimes my best "lessons" and my best "teachable moments" were when I did not say a word!

During a lecture, a student got up from his desk, walked to the Kleenex box on my desk, grabbed a tissue and went back to his desk. I didn't think anything of it until a girl shrieked and pointed at a trail of blood from the student's seat to the Kleenex box. I looked at the boy who was holding a tissue over his nose and said, "Go to the nurse."

He said, "No."

I raised my voice and said again, "Go to the nurse!"

There were drops of blood everywhere. He stood up tall and stated respectfully: "I do not want to be denied my educational opportunity."

How many of us would jump at any opportunity to leave the classroom? How many of us would want to stay and not forgo their educational opportunity?

Hmm, I wonder. Beyond the Lesson Plan.

We need to all wonder, "What is my role?" We need to know our responsibilities.

When Ben Franklin walked out of the Constitutional Convention—remember, they had met in complete secrecy—he was greeted by a crowd yelling, "Dr. Franklin, what kind of government do we get?" His reply was simple and concise yet brilliant. "A republic, if you can keep it."

What revitalizes your faith in the great American experiment in representative democracy?

Freedom is not free. Indeed!

For my first film night, I showed *Saving Private Ryan*. The auditorium was filled with students who had just filled up on pizza and were ramped up on Mountain Dew. They were talking and screwing around and acting like teenagers who were having a good time. The auditorium was loud and filled with tomfoolery. It was my very first film night, and it was looking like it might be my last. But the moment the film began, you could have heard a pin drop. They were mesmerized. When it ended, the audience sat in complete silence.

I would continue to have film nights for the rest of my teaching career. I believe one of the great scenes in film history occurs when Private Ryan is told by Captain Miller to "Earn This!" As students began filing out of the auditorium thanking me, I would remind them to "Earn This!" Earn what your country has done for you. Earn what your ancestors have done for you. Make your descendants proud of you. As the saying goes: Pay it Forward!

Waving my outstretched arms that night, I asked my students, "Have you earned this?" I find myself asking almost every day, "Have I earned this?"

# 29. How do you engage in political efficacy and civic virtue?

As I write this, it has been four years since I decided to retire after thirty-three years of teaching American government and American history to high school students and begin my run for the Minnesota State Senate. For years I told my students and my colleagues that I loved my job, that I would never retire, and that they would have to carry me out of my classroom in a coffin.

God, I loved teaching!

In April, 2015, I found myself at a Planning for Retirement orientation. My wife for years had tried to get me to get a financial plan for our future. I always resisted because I was never going to retire. During the orientation, they told me I could retire at the end of the 2015–2016 school year. I said, "Sign me up." My wife was shocked. My colleagues and friends were shocked. What came over me that day, I will never know. But I was going to begin the most memorable year-and-a-half of my life.

So, I began my last year teaching like every year of my career, with one exception. Over the summer, I printed 172 three-inch buttons, each containing a handwritten number from 1 to 172 on the front with enough room on the back for a brief handwritten note. I had decided to wear a button every day with the number of school days prominently displayed on the front. Every day I would write on the back, "Thank you for your political efficacy and civic virtue. Cwod" (in permanent marker.) Then I'd hand that button to the student who exhibited extra effort and enthusiasm for life that deserved to be acknowledged.

I gave these buttons out to remind me of the human potential in all of us, including the students who made me a better teacher, made me a better person or made those around them a little richer and wiser. I wanted to seek out the best in my students. I wanted to focus on their strengths rather than their weaknesses. I soon realized that I could have used a lot more buttons!

I began my first and only blog by posting the following on the World Wide Web:

"This is my last year teaching and it has been a wonderful thirty-three years. I have made 172 buttons beginning with number 172, which I wore on the first day of school, counting down to 1, which I will wear on the last day of school. I am not counting down the days—far from it. I am reminding myself every day that I only have 172, or 119 or 43 days left to make the most of every day, to cherish the moments. In short, Memento Mori. I do not want to take the "senior (citizen) slide." I never want to squander a single moment of my existence. I want my students and my peers to know I am giving 100% every single day."

The following are some examples of my last 172 days.

Day 146—to the student who came up to me after class asking if the milk glass was my "ROSEBUD" (see Citizen Kane). I had just told the class about how I had been given a milk glass by my immigrant grandmother when I was five years old with the JFK quote on it: "Ask not what your country can do for you; ask what you can do for your country." The milk glass had been lost until a student explaiined how I could find it on e-Bay, which I did. I found my ROSEBUD!

Day 132—to the first student, who I had not had in class, who brought a button "number 163" that she had found in the commons and knew I would know who had lost it. I repeat, she found button 163 and could have left it there, could have wrecked it, could have tossed it, but she knew it meant a lot to someone. Amazing!

Day 124—to the student to whom, before lunch, I recommended a book she should read if she was finding today's lesson interesting.

When I came back from lunch, she was sitting in my room reading the book rather than going to eat.

Day 121—to the student who stuck around after class to say "Thank you," and who, when I said thanks back, said, "No, really, thank you for today." He really wanted to let me know today was special for him.

Day 108—to the student that had the chutzpah to "shshsh" her peers who were talking while someone else was sharing her thoughts to the class. She also took the initiative to answer the phone when she knew I was too busy.

Day 99—to the student who reached down and shut off his phone when it rang. But what was truly amazing—she did not look down to see who it was. She simply reached down and shut it off without taking her eyes off the lesson. A "class" act.

Day 85—to the student who wanted to "high five" after class, and who told him I didn't do that. When he offered a "fist bump," and I told him I didn't do that either. When he asked me what I did, I told him "I pinky promise." Since then, he has pinky promised me every day as he walks out of class.

Day 72—for one of the most generous and gracious things I have seen this year. A student needed a stamp for the letter they were turning in for me to send to their representative. A young woman announced, "I have an extra stamp," and offered it to the student she did not even know.

Day 60—to the student that sent me an email thanking me for the "inspiring lesson" from earlier that day. This came to me at a time when I was not having my best day, and I thought my lesson had not reached anyone.

Day 48—to the student who went home every day and taught her father the lessons from class. Her father was preparing to become a US citizen.

Day 34—to the student who has so many problems in her personal life, yet gave me a thoughtful and generous gift that meant so much to me. I am amazed at those who are so "troubled" and yet still think about others.

Day 25—to the student who on senior skip day—when most students were not in class—remained engaged. With only ten students in class, I let the students have some study time. All immediately got out their computers and plugged in headphones to tune out school. This young lady decided to spend the time reading all the "stuff" on my walls.

Day 20—to the student who may very well have done one of the most amazing things ever. When I jokingly asked if anyone had AAA batteries for my clicker, he dug through his backpack and removed the batteries from his calculator so I could continue the PowerPoint.

I wish I had done this activity every single year of my teaching career. I would recommend it to anyone retiring or ending their tenure. In fact, I would recommend to anyone beginning their career. Doing something helps to remain focused on why we are all here.

Now as a state senator, I get to listen to those same thirsty and hungry minds. My students are now constituents, lobbyists, government employees and citizens. They are now trying to leave the world a little bit better than it was yesterday.

I believe that an educated, informed, enlightened and engaged population is a necessary ingredient for every democracy to properly function. That civic virtue and political efficacy go hand in hand.

After my election to the Minnesota State Senate, I came to discover that the Minnesota State Constitution states in Article XIII: "The stability of a republican form of government depending mainly upon the intelligence of the people, it is the duty of the legislature to establish a general and uniform system of public schools."

My only constitutional duty as a state senator is to see that we have an intelligent citizenry in order to have stability in our republican form of government—a duty I do not take lightly.

Civic virtue is displaying the personal attributes associated with civil and political order.

Political efficacy is knowing that you can and will make a difference in political affairs.

Civic duty is knowing and displaying a combined and robust sense of civic virtue and political efficacy.

# 30. Have you become great at what you are good at?

I used to love analyzing and discussing with my students why, according to *Time* magazine, Albert Einstein was Person of the Century. I remind my students that at one time he was just like them, sitting at his desk and wondering what the gods had in store for him. What will be your destiny, Luke?

We all can't do great and momentous things. But what we all can do is great and momentous things in our own unique way. We can set out to leave this universe grander than we came upon it.

We the people have done a great deal of good as a nation. We have certainly left our mark on humanity. We have given humanity engineering feats and marvels of science that truly will stand the test of time. We have sent Americans to the moon and to the bottom of the oceans. We have preserved our natural wonders and developed our natural resources. Our ideas and institutions have revolutionized the world. Yet there is so much more to do.

I often would go on faux field trips during class. I'd announce that we were are going on a "field trip." Students get very excited, and I'd tell them to leave their parental permission slips on my desk as we begin to leave the classroom. I would get a few panicky looks by students wondering, "When did he pass out permission slips?" This always cracked me up.

Then I'd start singing, "The wheels on the bus go round and round" and "The windshield wipers go swish, swish, swish," until we arrived at our destination, which was always a poster or a print on my wall that I wanted the students to see up close. To the students who thought we were leaving the room on a real field trip, it was always a major disappointment.

Every year in December, I asked my students who would be *Time's* Person of the Year. After I got a few ideas from the class, we'd head out on another "field trip" to the front of the room where I had hung the original cover of every *Time's* Person of the Year since my first year of teaching in 1983. Alongside the covers was a poster of every winner since 1927. We'd discuss all the winners—Lindbergh, Roosevelt, Queen Elizabeth, Gorbachev and more. We'd discuss the more recent winners—Bush, Zuckerberg, the Ebola Doctors and Obama. I would tell them that the honor goes to the "person or persons who had the greatest impact on our planet that year."

Then I would challenge them by asking, "Who among you will be a consideration for this highest of honors?"

Will you solve the puzzle? Will you get to the summit and show us the way? What will your accomplishment be? What will be your capstone? WILL STUDENTS SOMEDAY WRITE ESSAYS ABOUT YOU? Who do you believe will be the Person of the Twenty-first Century?

Could it be you?

What are you good at?

What are you great at?

What are you going to be the best at, something no one can do better?

What is your purpose?

What is your calling?

What will be your legacy?

Make an impact that will be felt long after you have left! Will anyone utter your name a hundred years from now?

Once I told my students to get out of their seats and come up the front of the class for another "field trip." I proceeded to go through

174

four paintings by Thomas Cole called the *Voyage of Life* from the National Gallery of Art. "To get personal with the paintings, you really need to be up front," I said. "Up close and face to face with the painting."

The first painting shows a young baby in a small watercraft leaving a cave (the womb). An hourglass situated in the bow is completely full, and a guardian angel is looking over the child. The child is surrounded by beautiful flora and fauna and a bright blue sky—a beautiful future indeed.

The second painting is more relevant and pertinent to my students. An eighteen-year-old youth is heading out alone in a boat. The guardian angel is leaving for the first time since birth. The youth has his hand up as if calling to the object he is heading for. The hourglass is emptier now as the youth heads toward Shangri-La (or paradise, utopia, Eden, Atlantis, Eldorado or whatever you wish to call that place for which all youth been searching since we crawled out of the oceans)— that shining city upon the hill. This is the More Perfect Union our forefathers wrote about. Some say we will never get there, and some say it is only a dream, a fantasy. However, everything humanity has accomplished began with a simple dream.

As I pointed to the youth heading up the path to his future, I told the students that they are so preoccupied with watching screens and viral videos, or the video game du jour—that they fail to get off the boat and now are heading toward a Soma-induced future. I explained that they, my students, had totally missed getting off the boat, so now the boat turned and their utopia was now behind them.

The third painting was frightening. In it, the youth has become middle-aged like me. The figure was headed toward chaos and impending doom. The hourglass was winding down. The man was praying as he moved towards a waterfall surrounded by demonic creatures. The fears it provokes are, "Where am I going?" "How did I get here?" "I have a mortgage, a car payment, thankless kids, a miserable marriage, and a boss who does not appreciate me." "Everything is broken. Everything is dark. Everything is utterly hopeless."

The fourth and final painting shows an old man in a battered boat. Usually a student would say, "Are you sure, Mr. Cwodzinsk,i that this figure in the painting is not you?" The hourglass is gone and waters are calm as the figure reflects on: "Where?" "How did I get here?" "What did I miss?" "Did I do what I set out to do?" His guardian angel greets him at the end of his journey. He reflects on his accomplishments, failures and regrets. The puzzle pieces he failed to find and affix to the bigger puzzle will now have to be completed by others, if at all. "Did I find my purpose?" "Did I achieve my capstone?" "Is the piece of the puzzle I solved a pivotal piece that connected all the other pieces?"

Shangri-La, paradise, utopia, Eden, Atlantis, Eldorado, whatever you want to call the place—how are you going to help us all get there?

Then I asked my students why there were so many films and books depicting dystopias rather than utopias? How is that helpful? What does it say about human nature? Why, in the depictions of dystopias, are the masses lacking any attributes of individualism and citizenry? Why did they submit to the machine?

It is then that I returned to the second painting and asked the students if they were ready for this. "How are you not going to become the person in the third painting?" As I showed them painting three, I asked, "Is it inevitable that we all end up with a miserable and meaningless life?" I then announced, "The field trip is over, let's get back on the bus—go back to your seats!" And then I sang, "The wheels on the bus go round and round, round and round, round and round. The windshield wipers go swish swish swish."

Sometimes, after one of these "faux field trips," a student would ask if we ever went on a real field trip as part of this class?

I would say, "Regrettably, no. One year I took students on a field trip to a deserted island, but that year we became stranded for weeks. No one knew where we were, and then one day, students found a bottle washed up on the beach. Everyone ran toward it, and when they opened the bottle, a Genie came out. He said, 'I grant you three wishes.' Being the only adult, I suggested, "OK, all the liberals get one, all the conservatives get one, and I get one.'

"So, the liberals gathered on my left yelled out: "We miss our families and school—we wish we were back home." And Poof! They were gone. The conservatives gathered on my right yelled out, "We miss our families and school—we wish we were back home." And Poof! They were gone. So, I stood there alone, stranded on the deserted island. I looked at the Genie, I looked to my left, I looked to my right. Then, with a saddened expression, I said, "I already miss those guys, I wish they were back here. And Poof!"

But I digress.

If you wanted to avoid the third painting, you would need to figure out what you are good at and become great at it. Perhaps the best at it. Who knows, you might even be *Time* magazine's Person of the Year.

And why would you have been picked? Because you were simply the greatest at it!

# 31. Have you left the world better than when you came upon it?

The Eden Prairie senior class votes on which teacher should deliver the commencement speech at graduation. A few times I was given that honor. This always meant a great deal to me, not only because the senior class wanted my thoughts to be the last ones they would hear before graduation, but also because those thoughts came from someone who was unable to attend his own high school graduation.

My first commencement speech was one of my proudest moments. My mom and dad were proud of their son, who had been such a headache throughout his own school career a few years earlier. In a hospital bed near death, I had denied them the opportunity to see their only child receive his diploma. Ten years later, they watched me handing diplomas out to high school graduates with 5,000 in attendance. That was quite a night.

The program at one of these commencement ceremonies stated, "Closing Remarks: Steve Cwodzinski." I thought this was interesting, because all through school my teachers would say: "No more remarks out of you, Steve."

The minute I rose to deliver my first speech, some fool began to talk. I opened by saying, "Before I begin my speech, I have something important to say." I thought it was funny, but no one laughed. I was talking about my philosophy of life, and someone shouted, "Who writes your immaterial?" But I digress.

My first commencement speech was at Eden Prairie High School in 1988. I opened by declaring that in "EPHS," the acronym that makes up our high school's identity, can be found the meaning of life. I dedicated my theory to the graduates:

Exploration
Purpose
Happiness
Success

Life is like a pyramid. It consists of a base of all our experiences. The more we Explore, the more experiences we have and the larger our base becomes. As our base grows with each new experience, it becomes increasingly easier to figure out what our Purpose is—our reason for being. How will we contribute our individual uniquenesses to the common good? Once we find our Purpose, we can achieve a true measure of Happiness, realizing the joys and pleasures of our existence, which may be the ultimate in Success. Through our Success, climbing to the summit of the pyramid, we begin illuminating the way for ourselves and others, thus helping us all find our own meaning of Success.

The happiest people I know are constantly Exploring, giving their life a Purpose, which of course brings Happiness. Your achievements, accomplishments, and triumphs come as a result of a life full of Exploring, having a Purpose, and finding Happiness. The end result: A Successful Life.

This is what I told the graduates. I then read my favorite poem.

## What Is Success? by Ralph Waldo Emerson

"To laugh often and much; to win the respect of intelligent people and the affection of children; to earn the appreciation of honest critics and endure the betrayal of false friends; to appreciate the beauty; to find the best in others; to leave the world a bit better, whether by a healthy child, a garden patch or a redeemed social condition; to know even one life has breathed easier because you have lived. This is to have succeeded!"

I then read my favorite poem written by me.

179

## **Success!**

### By Steve Cwodzinski

We set out to Explore
We unearth our Purpose
We find Happiness
Success!

Go get a piece of paper right now. I will wait. GO!

Draw an unfinished pyramid similar to the one found on the back of the one-dollar bill. Leave it unfinished. At the base of the pyramid, put the year you were born. (For me, it was MCMLVIII: 1958. Use Roman Numerals—it will be fun). This is your Cornerstone, your foundation.

Now, draw the stones that make up your transformative moments. Your milestones, your stepping stones, and your keystones.

Your milestones may be your first day of school, your graduation, the day you volunteered your time, when you learned to play a musical instrument or learned a second language, your first promotion, your first kiss, your first child. Then document your steppingstones, which got you to the next level. You are, after all, as irreplaceable and unique as your fingerprints. On the day you were born you were "a new order for the ages"

As I said earlier, Mark Twain stated, "The two most important days in a person's life were the day they were born (your cornerstone) and the day they figured out why? (your capstone)

At one time, all the people that came before you were sitting in a cave, or at a desk, or in a cubicle, or at a kitchen table, or at an assembly line, or entering New York City on a steamship. They all wondered, "What will be my legacy, my contribution, my footprint?" They dreamed of great things. They were searching for their purpose.

So, what is your purpose?

Will you be among those that climbed to the summit of humanity? To finish your pyramid? Or maybe your pyramid remains unfinished because you are never truly satisfied with your quest for perfection.

You are, after all, following some great steppingstones. They are

180

everywhere if you look. There are stepping stones left for you by Martin Luther King and George Washington. There are steppingstones left for you by Albert Einstein and Susan B. Anthony. There are stepping stones left for you by your parents, teachers, grandparents and your friends. These are powerful and memorable stones, indeed. But in order to leave your own imprint, your steppingstone, you need to step up and walk your own way—to climb forward, outward, and upward, to set your own milestones. Yes, and maybe even a capstone.

Hopefully, you will achieve your capstone before arriving at your Gravestone!

Your life's mission—your capstone—is the completion of your pyramid before you pass. Of the over eighty billion people who have lived on this planet, I doubt the dying words of very many were: "I found my purpose, I finished, I solved all the pieces of the puzzle, my pyramid is complete!" All any of us can do is solve as much of the puzzle, gettting a little bit closer to that more perfect union, before we pass on. Our purpose in life is having a purpose bigger than ourselves—TO HAVE FIGURED IT OUT!

The past and the present are filled with acts of greatness that make up that human pyramid—the momentous milestones, steppingstones and keystones that made us who we are. Our national pyramid was built by explorers, wanderers, adventure seekers and risk-takers. They left their marks—now it is your turn. ON YOUR MARK, GET SET, GO!

Leave your world a little bit better than when you came upon it. Truly!

This is my philosophy of life. Most of the best lessons I ever taught—those teachable moments—were the ones that were never part of any lesson plan. What I tried to teach my students for thirty-three years was that the more we explore and wander, the more likely we will arrive at our purpose, our reason for being, which results in states of happiness and joyfulness, ultimately leading to a successful existence.

This was my lesson plan!

So, I ask:

How do you define success?

How will you get there?

What will be the grand scheme to your existence?

What do the gods have in store for you?

Mark Twain said, "The two most important days in a person's life are the day they were born and the day they figured out why." Most likely, if you are reading this, you have already accomplished the former. Now, on to the latter.

Figure out why you were born and leave this world a little bit better than when you came upon it. That is why we are all here.

# 32. How much of the puzzle have you solved?

Solve as much of the puzzle as possible before you pass on to the next thing.

I used to show four slides in class. The first one showed a photo of a very brave, young girl, Ruby Bridges, surrounded by federal marshals as she was about to walk off to an all-white school. When the painter Norman Rockwell saw the photo, it inspired him to paint his masterpiece, *The Problem We All Live With*. The actual painting is my second slide.

The third slide shows the lyrics to the Beatles song *Blackbird*—which I would then play. When Paul McCartney saw the painting by Rockwell, he penned this masterpiece. The Beatles captured perfectly the whimsical and magical moments a young girl undergoes as she walks to school, the rhythm and beat of every footstep. The lyrics are perfect:

Blackbird singing in the dead of night
Take these broken wings and learn to fly
All your life
You were only waiting for this moment to arise

I would sing out these lines, and then shout out:

What moment was the "Blackbird" waiting to arise?
What moment are you waiting to arise?

The fourth slide shows a photo of a much older Ruby Bridges (who was then around my age) standing alongside President Obama. They are in the White House standing in front of Rockwell's painting, which Obama had hung in the White House.

Ruby Bridges, a six-year-old girl, had inspired a photographer, who had inspired a painter, who had inspired a composer, who had inspired a president, who had inspired us all.

The importance of the education of our youth—indeed!

Then I would show a slide of Mary Beth Tinker and her black arm-band. That arm-band is on display in the Newseum in DC. She had worn the black arm band to school in her demonstration against the Vietnam War, even though the principal had told her not to wear it. She said she had a right to wear it under the First Amendment. The principal disagreed. Her case made it all the way to the Supreme Court in Tinker vs Des Moines. In that case, the court declared, "Students do not shed their constitutional rights at the school-house gate."

Then I would ask: "Will anything of yours ever end up in a museum?"

Will we want to preserve an artifact of yours for all time?

Will your acts of civic engagement or civil disobedience be worth preserving for others to be inspired by?

I ended with a slide of Malala, who at seventeen had just won the Nobel Peace Prize. She survived an attempted murder for the crime of going to school.

I would then ask my class: "What have you done?" Pointing to myself, I'd ask: "What have I done?" I have taught many young people like Malala who wanted to learn.

Our purpose on this planet is to solve as much of the puzzle as possible before we pass. To leave the world a better place than we found it. To solve a piece or two of the puzzle in the little time we have.

Einstein was once asked, "What is the meaning of life?" He replie,: "To solve as much of the puzzle as possible before you pass." He practiced what he preached.

I have cited this quote by Einstein in class for years. When my students cite the quote in their English classes, their teachers ask them to back it up. No one has ever been able to find Einstein actually saying these words. Some students have even found my name on the Internet as the original source of the quote. This leads me to think I may have coined that phrase myself and credited it to Einstein. We need more research on this.

Then I ask the students. when 2099 arrives and names are kicked around for Person of the Twenty-first Century, will they be on the short list? After a long pause, I ask: "Why not you?" It will most likely go to the person who solves the greatest puzzle pieces of the this century.

I recently bought a jig-saw puzzle that I finished in a weekend. I was so proud of myself. The box said ages 6-10 years. But I digress.

How much of the puzzle do you think you have solved?

Which puzzle piece are you most proud of?

If you could solve just one puzzle piece, what would that piece be?

To solve as much of the puzzle as possible before you pass, indeed!

I let those words soak in for a little while and then I remind students that:

We all can't build bridges or discover new worlds.

We all can't find a cure for cancer or solve the problems of poverty.

We all can't be president, prophets. poets and playwrights.

We all can't do great things resulting in our receiving honors and awards and accolades and recognition. We cannot all climb to the summit of humanity and shout out to the rest of us, "Wake up!"

We cannot all be Person of the Century, or Person of the Year, or make it onto their cover.

But what we all can do are small things in our own unique way.

We can all solve one little piece of the puzzle, or two, or three, or.......

Our own puzzle knows no boundaries or borders, it is only limited by our imaginations.

Solving just one piece of the puzzle during our brief time—that would be excellence.

That would be sublime.
That would be success.
You can make an impact that will be felt!
You can stir up an idea that will last a thousand years!
In your search for meaning.
In your journey for Exploration.
In your search for a Purpose.
In your pursuit of Happiness.
In your quest for Success.
To the summit of humanity!
Solve as much of the puzzle as possible before you pass on to the next thing.
Truly!

# 33. Where are you taking your celestial spark?

Take your celestial spark around the world and Let it Shine! Let it Shine! Let it Shine!

I always ended my courses with the following story:

When my daughter and son were little, they begged us to take them to see Raffi, their favorite singer/songwriter. I told them I'd take them to see Springsteen, Prince or Dylan, but I would not sit through two hours of *Baby Beluga, Banana Phone* and *Joshua Giraffe*. My wife said the kids really wanted to see Raffi, and it would be a new experience for all of us. And then she gave me that look of hers that meant, "We are going no matter what you might say." So, we went.

Well, as things turned out, it was one of the best concerts I'd ever attended. I sat with a smile on my face for two hours. How can you not love hearing three thousand kids screaming to *Banana Phone* and *The Deep Blue Sea*. Every song was about joy and happiness, about taking positive chances and positive risks, about animals and circuses and balloons and ponies.

And then Raffi said thank you and walked off the stage. Thousands of screaming kids—and I admit, a parent or two—chanted RAFFI! RAFFI! RAFFI! until Raffi reappeared on stage and shouted, "Ok, boys and girls, give me the finger!"

I looked around. What finger was Raffi going to get? I could never say, "Give me the finger!" to high school students. Yet that is not the finger Raffi received. Thousands of five-year-olds raised their index fingers to the sky and started singing with Raffi, "I'm going to take this light around the world and I'm going to let it shine, let it shine, let I shine. I'm going to take this light of mine around the world and I'm going to let it shine, let it shine, let it shine."

I watched the crowd, my goose bumps growing by the second. As the children's refrain continued, I began to think about the Greek philosopher Plato who once said, "Those having torches will pass them on to others."

Take your light, nay your torch, around the world and let it shine, let it shine, let it shine.

Shine the way for you and all those around you.

Do you know how Noah saw where he was going at night? He used floodlights! But, for the very last time, I digress!

No matter how small or grand you perceive it, you can set out to leave this world better than it was when you came upon it. You can make an impact that will be felt long after you are gone.

What will be your life's defining quest?

When people have a near-death experience, they always talk about seeing a bright, blinding light. Steve Jobs' dying words were, "Oh my, oh my, oh my." What was he seeing? Artists depict a halo around the prophets. What is that circle of light? What was that fire/light that the gods did not want Prometheus to have? Those that saw Lincoln during the last week of his life describe him as if there was a "physical radiance" about him. When your mother was pregnant with you, people told her that she "glowed!" Go ahead, ask her!

What is this light? For thousands of years, philosophers have pondered , the meaning of this light that emanates from each of us. For some, that light is a flicker, for others it is a glow, for still others it is a steady light, and for some it is a beacon.

YOU can truly illuminate this world. Yes, YOU can lead US out of any darkness.

Let us all begin to TAP THAT LIGHT!

Take your torch and make it a lightning bolt of action and a beacon of light for all the world to see.

Let your heart become a beacon of kindness for those who are angry and enraged.

Let your soul become a lighthouse for those who are lost and struggling.

Let your celestial spark be a lightning bolt of action during troubling times.

Let us all pass our torches on to our posterity, and all leave the world a little bit better than we found it.

This is what defines us.

This is what unites us,

that light emanating from your spirit.

It is our hearts,

Our universal conscience,

That celestial spark.

It is that fire in your belly and that glow in your heart and that blaze in your soul.

Today, among us is a future diplomat that will bring peace to a troubled region.

Today, among us is a scientist that will cure cancer.

Today, among us is a social worker who will bring joy to a troubled family.

Today, among us is a children's writer who will be the next Dr. Suess.

When they are asked, "How did you do it?" let their answer be: "It all began with a torch that was passed on to me."

Let us all pass our torches on to our posterity, and all leave the world a little better than we found it.

Over my thirty-three years of teaching, I tried to pass my torch on to others. Now I have retired from teaching and have begun the next phase of my life as a Minnesota state senator representing the communities of Eden Prairie and Minnetonka.

Every day, as I walk up that grand staircase and I enter the Senate Chambers, I walk beneath a mural high above the entrance. The mural is allegorical and depicts three women, with a Latin word next to each figure. One is crouched by a fire depicting the past (Hodi), where she

189

has just made a torch. The middle figure stands in the center holding that torch high over her head. She depicts the present (Heri). The torch is being handed by the middle figure to a third depicting the future (Cras). It is for the third figure that I wrote this book.

Take your celestial spark around the world and Let it Shine! Let it Shine! Let it Shine!

Truly.

# Acknowledgements

I would like to thank my most ardent and critical editor—my wife, Patti—as well as my children Erica and John, and my son-in-law Matt. They have been listening to me talk about this book for five years. Next, I would like to thank the numerous friends who were part of this process: Dave Knudson, Dave Page, Megan Gernes Maynor, Viv Miller, and Paul Klauda. Thanks also to all my colleagues who inspired me throughout my career; I would not be who I am without any of you. Also, I must acknowledge the professionals at Calumet Editions: editor Gary Lindberg and publisher Ian Graham Leask. Gentlemen, it was pure pleasure working with you. Lastly, I would like to thank the twelve thousand students who made this book possible.

# About the Author

Steve was raised in Superior, Wisconsin. While attending the University of Minnesota, he met his wife, Patti. They have two adult children. Steve spent more than thirty years teaching American Government and American History. He challenged more than 12,000 students to think for themselves and find empowerment with an advanced sense of political efficacy and civic duty. Steve received numerous awards including: Eden Prairie's Teacher of the Year, Minnesota finalist for Teacher of the Year, Presidential Scholar's Influential Teacher, and the Distinguished Teacher Award from the US Congress. After retiring from teaching in 2016, he took the opportunity to enhance his own political efficacy and civic virtue. He ran for public office, winning a seat in the Minnesota State Senate. Steve is excited to promote the same values in the senate that he had advocated for in the classroom.